THE WARREN COURT AND ITS CRITICS

THE WARREN COURT
&
ITS CRITICS

CLIFFORD M. LYTLE

THE UNIVERSITY OF ARIZONA PRESS
TUCSON, ARIZONA

About the Author . . .

CLIFFORD M. LYTLE became head of the Department of Government at the University of Arizona in 1969. He is a political scientist with special interest in civil liberties, constitutional law, and the judicial process — all topics on which he writes frequently for legal and academic journals. Holder of an LL.B. degree from Western Reserve Law School, he practiced law in Ohio and is a member of the Ohio State Bar. He later received the Ph.D. degree from the University of Pittsburgh.

First printing 1968
Second printing 1970

THE UNIVERSITY OF ARIZONA PRESS

S. B. N. 8165-0099-1
L. C. No. 66-28788

TO DAVID ONG

FOREWORD

Supreme Court criticism is like literary criticism; the style and the viewpoint may change but the flood goes on forever. Take style. There is the hot invective — "A most monstrous and unexampled decision . . . the zenith of despotic power," said Roane of *Cohens v. Virginia* in 1821. There is the whiff of subversion — Jefferson's "subtle corps of sappers and miners constantly working underground to undermine the foundations of our confederated fabric" in 1820 is only a somewhat more elegant version of a 1960 critic quoted by Professor Lytle who denounces the Court's "demolition job on the Constitution."

There is the light touch masking the hard blow — Lincoln's Dred Scott banter about "Stephen, Franklin, Roger and James, for instance." There is learned talk. There is also superior talk, of which I may have been guilty myself on occasion but as to which, as Professor Lytle develops, Professors Hart, Bickel, and Wellington take all recent nose-in-the-air honors. But whatever the tone, there is always criticism.

Not only does the style of the brick but also the vantage point of the brick thrower change over the years. Lincoln snicked the Court on its attitude toward slavery, old Bob LaFollette and Theodore Roosevelt for its sanctification of business. FDR went after the Court for its "horse and buggy" transportation of his reforms to the junk heap, the Country's conservatives leaped to defend the Court he attacked.

But lawyers are agile by profession. In more recent years, to borrow a line from Walton Hamilton apropos of a different legal shift, "As the situation demanded, the two combatants exchanged position, legal weapons, and arguments." When, after the appointment of Chief Justice Warren, the Court moved in a generally liberal direction, the old defenders dropped their shields and took up their bludgeons. In the happy early days of the American Bar Association, Southern lawyers had been the moving spirits in that association's fine gentlemen's club at Saratoga Springs and had taken the group into politics for the first time to oppose recall of judges. By the 1950's, some of their grandsons couldn't get out the "Impeach Earl Warren" circulars fast enough, and Supreme Court Justices might well have suffered physical violence had they paused to visit in some Southern locales. The free speech, fair trial, church and state, and Congressional and legislative redistricting decisions unleashed a series of storms which swirled together into a first-class blow.

Professor Lytle has done the present a favor and the future a great service by collecting, classifying, and commenting on these criticisms of our own day. He has undertaken the job as a political scientist seeking to bring "analytical order out of this political chaos" to create what he calls "a manageable framework."

This he has done. If any other work makes any serious effort to think through the structure of criticism, I have not seen it. But I must ask Professor Lytle to forgive me in saying that he grossly underestimates the value of his book, which I believe deserves its greatest accolade as a history; and I hope it may be so used, classified, and reviewed. This is a remarkable collection of a decade of criticism, criticism in Congress, in the press, in the pulpit — yes, and in the sewer, too, for a fine collection of Billingsgate is included here. Underneath the petty and the inflamed, one can hear a touch of genuine anguish as a generation and a people forced to change its ways reluctantly accommodate to what seems to them a new and unwarranted order.

This book will be useful to general historians of the latter twentieth century. It will be invaluable to Court historians and judicial biographers. I personally find the detailed account of Congressional proposals and attitudes particularly informing.

Court criticism, as it is customary to say somewhat sanctimoniously in discussions of this subject, is highly desirable; no institution is served by being above criticism. As 175 years of experience show, the Court does not really need to fear being unduly idolized; the critics are always with us. Their comments would be more constructive, as Justice Brennan observed in 1963, after an unduly heavy spate of remarkably uninformed criticism of a school prayer decision, if the critics would read the decisions first; the flood of hostility started in that case within two hours of the announcement of lengthy opinions, before they could possibly have been considered. The Court's recent change in its age-old custom of announcing all opinions on Monday, spreading them through the week instead, is in part intended to meet this very problem by not giving out all at once more than can possibly be considered before the next press deadline.

By this simple adjustment, the Court will perhaps protect itself. The Justices, if they can withstand a sense of depression from seeing so many massed misunderstandings, can perhaps work still further to protect the institution they serve by contemplating Professor Lytle's collection.

John P. Frank
Phoenix, Arizona

PREFACE

One of the more fascinating conflicts on the current political hori-
zon was generated by a series of controversial decisions issuing from
the Supreme Court of the United States. The reaction to these decisions,
especially in conservative circles, has been rather startling. It has been
characterized by anger, fear, and often frustration. More importantly,
it has set in motion a continuing barrage of criticism directed toward the
Court and its personnel.

The criticism levied at the Warren Court has taken on many
shapes and forms. Flowing from a number of different sources, it has
been varied in nature, running the gamut from "reasoned appeal" to
spontaneous irrational outburst. This study is an attempt to bring a
degree of analytical order to this political chaos — to project the
attacks upon the Court into a manageable framework so that they may
be better understood. The scope of the investigation is limited to a
period beginning in 1954 with the rendering of the School Segregation
Cases and running up to and including the year 1961. It was during
these years that the battles were most vigorously waged. The more
significant controversial cases decided since 1961, such as the School
Prayer decision, the right-to-counsel cases, and the legislative apportionment cases, have also been included to make the analysis as current
as possible.

The author wishes to thank the *Journal of Public Law* for the use
of material which appeared initially in an article in that publication,
Vol. XII, No. 2 (1963), pp. 290-312.

The task of writing this analysis was made considerably easier by
the assistance from a number of generous friends and colleagues. In
particular my thoughts turn to Holbert Carroll, Carl Beck, Edward

Cooke, Morris Ogul, and Samuel Hays who helped me to launch the project. The thoughtful comments and suggestions of Currin Shields, David Bingham, Harold Rhodes, and C. Oscar Jones provided immeasurable assistance. I also wish to acknowledge my debt to the Mellon Foundation of the University of Pittsburgh, and the Institute of Government Research of the University of Arizona, for financial support, and to thank the University of Arizona Press for effecting publication of the book. Finally, special mention must be made of my wife, Biz, who guarded the manuscript from the possible extra-curricular editing of my three children, Christian, Carrie, and Jamie Scott.

Clifford M. Lytle
Tucson, Arizona

CONTENTS

THE WARREN COURT AND ITS CRITICS

1. THE COURT AS A TARGET OF CRITICISM

During the first decade of Earl Warren's leadership of the Supreme Court, the Chief Justice and his colleagues were the objects of repeated criticism from a wide variety of critics within the public and private sector. Some of these comments have been well reasoned. But often the attacks have been conspicuous for vitriolic and irrational overtones.

Illustrative of this is an outburst from Marine Colonel Mitchell Paige to a patriotic gathering known as Project Alert in December, 1961. Paige noted that although some people wanted to impeach Chief Justice Warren, "hanging would be more deserved."[1]

Levying attacks on the judiciary is far from a new game. Indeed, even a casual acquaintance with American history reveals that the Court has often been the focal point of bitter controversy. Yet for some reason this fact never seemed to register on the American public, indoctrinated as it was with the idea that the high tribunal should enjoy a sanctity not unlike that of the British Crown. The voicing of such attacks upon the Court probably has moved many people to reappraise their views.

The right to criticize the Supreme Court as well as any other political institution in America now is well established. It has been said that "every litigant has the right to proceed from the courthouse, take his stand in the middle of the big road, and cuss the court." As Justice Brewer has phrased it, "many criticisms may be, like their authors, devoid of good taste, but better all sorts of criticism than no criticism at all. The moving waters are full of life and health; only in the still waters is stagnation and death."[2]

In spite of Justice Brewer's philosophy, the position of the Supreme Court in relation to political criticism is a rather extraordinary one.

1

Unlike other political institutions, the Court stands aloof from the political arena and consequently it has evolved into what Dean Griswold has termed a "perfect whipping boy."[3] It is little wonder that a number of our more adroit politicians have seized the opportunity to attack an institution which has the reputation of remaining silent to criticism. The defense of the Court has been left basically to academicians and members of the various bar associations, who in the past have been somewhat tardy and remiss.

Although numerous approaches may be taken to understanding the mass of criticism, two authors stand out as having made significant contributions. C. Herman Pritchett in *Congress Versus the Supreme Court*[4] attacked the problem from a substantive standpoint, with an acute analysis of the central issues of controversy. The other book which assists in gaining perspective on the conflict is Walter F. Murphy's *Congress and the Court*.[5] Here a meticulous job of research is combined with personal observation in a portrayal of the role of Congressional response to the Court's decisions and "to the stimuli of interest groups whose goals were affected by judicial action."[6] In spite of the excellence of these two approaches, there remains room for further analysis.

The present study analyzes the political criticism directed toward the Warren Court in three different ways. First, the criticism will be categorized according to *source*, to make more manageable the mass of broad, unrelated attacks on the judiciary. The second major objective will be to ascertain the *nature* of the criticism, or the diverse grounds upon which it is predicated, in order to gain the perspective needed for precise analysis. Finally, an effort will be made to *assess* the attacks upon the judiciary within a given analytic framework.

SOURCES

The attacks on the judiciary flow from five sources. Congress constitutes the first, having served not only in a primary role, but also as a channel for protest from other sources.[7]

Interest groups constitute the second major source. These include pressure groups, private association, and individuals who have evidenced a dislike for some of the Court's decisions. These critics have become especially vocal with the rise of so many "patriotic" societies intent on fighting the Communist menace — the John Birch Society, for example.

The third source of criticism is state governmental agencies. The continuing growth of national power has made itself felt most effectively on the states, and this has generated a good deal of harsh feeling. Gatherings such as the Conference of State Chief Justices, annual Governor's Conferences, and state political organs 'such as the Virginia Commission on Constitutional Government, have all generated much criticism.

The fourth category is made up of federal and state law enforcement agencies. The impetus behind these subtle attacks are opinions which have generated technical barriers that allegedly block the functions of these agencies.

Finally, criticism of the Court comes from members of professional legal societies such as the American Bar Association, judges and former members of the judiciary, and a small group of academicians.

To categorize the criticism broadly is in itself a rather easy task. The issue becomes more complex as an attempt is made to delve further into the problem and gain a better perspective of it by examining the nature of the criticism or the ground upon which it is predicated.

NATURE

In general the criticism rests on four grounds. The first and foremost may be referred to as a "discordant social philosophy." This is an ideological dissent which involves economic, political, sociological and psychological differences, and arises from those groups who disagree with particular judicial decision or set of decisions.

Another ground is "intra-governmental conflict." Division of power among the various branches of government has set in motion a struggle for power among the executive, legislative and judicial bodies, a struggle embracing also federal-state competition. An excellent legislative-judicial example of the conflict is revealed in Senator Jenner's (R. Ind.) proposal to curb the appellate jurisdiction of the Supreme Court. A number of senators in Congress felt that the Court's ruling in *Watkins v. United States*[8] was a direct affront to the power of the legislature to investigate. In order to recoup the ground lost under the *Watkins* decision (dealing with the pertinency of the questions propounded by the House Un-American Activities Committee), Congress initiated a bill which would have precluded the Supreme Court from reviewing certain actions of Congress in the future. Though such an intra-governmental struggle for power is not always conspicuous on the surface, it does constitute an important base for criticism.

Closely related to "intra-governmental conflict" is the criticism arising from "decisional obstruction." The focus of attention here, however, is not so much on a positive struggle for power as on the elimination of a functional obstruction. This type of attack generally stems from those governmental agencies which have been hindered in the full and free exercise of their functions as the result of certain Supreme Court decisions. The best illustration of this centers around the actions of the state and local law enforcement agencies. When the Court handed down its decision in *Mallory v. United States*,[9] providing that a confession was inadmissible into evidence if there was an unreasonable delay in arraigning the accused, a number of the law enforcement agencies acted as if they were completely incapable of apprehending criminals effectively in the future. The *Mallory* decision then, in preventing those agencies from more easily fulfilling their intended function, constituted a basis upon which to criticize the Court.

A final ground of criticism is essentially theoretical and concerns conflicting interpretations of the judicial process. The critics here are not concerned with the results but with the methods the Court uses in attaining them. This methodological group is primarily, though not exclusively, composed of professional groups and academicians.

ASSESSMENT

Evaluating anything as subjective as criticism is a rather delicate art. There are those who would say such assessment is impossible, or at best useless, since it entails so many value judgments. Yet a cursory glance at numerous articles on the overall subject reveals that the phrases "responsible criticism" and "reckless and irresponsible attacks" are not infrequent. Quite obviously it is impossible to eliminate value judgments in the process of evaluating; yet it seems feasible to temper the personal element by conducting the evaluation within a critical frame of reference.

Attacks on the Supreme Court have manifested themselves in two distinct forms which provide guidelines for evaluation. On the one hand the attack may be directed at a particular decision or trend of decisions, and can be labeled "result-oriented."[10] On the other hand the criticism may be aimed at the Court's institutionalized process and referred to as "process-oriented."

The result-oriented critics have been by far the greatest in number. This commentary generally takes the form of a dissent from a particular decision or group of decisions. Its utility is that it keeps testing the value and wisdom of particular decisions by challenging continuously whether the consequences are in tune with the realities and needs of the times. Thus the way is kept open for rectifying seemingly harsh results in some future decision.

Such criticism also helps to fulfill a need by releasing ideological frustrations resulting from particular decisions. Though there may be little if any possibility of reversal, at least those who have been ideologically offended can find some consolation in "cussing out the Court." Probably the best illustration of this would be much of the Southern reaction to the School Segregation decisions.

Not all result-oriented criticism can be classified as constructive, however. On numerous occasions it will be little more than an emotional or irrational outburst, distinguished by an additional factor such as exaggerating the result out of all proportion, or ignoring any analysis whatsoever of the disputed case.

It is not that dissent must be devoid of all emotional overtones, but some attacks are levied with such sweeping generalities that they reveal complete indifference and ignorance of the case in question. As former Attorney General William P. Rogers told an American Bar Association convention, such "sweeping generalizations and across-the-board condemnations of the courts...are not in the best interest of the nation."[11] And though criticism is essential to the mature functioning of our judiciary, it must be "informed criticism."

Bernard Schwartz has phrased it thus: "Criticism of the Court at the very least must be based upon understanding if it is to be fruitful."[12] It appears that today a number of Congressmen as well as other critics "prefer condemning the Court in public orations to taking constructive effort to remedy what they consider to be the Court's errors."[13] This approach, as further developed, is especially prevalent among those critics who have become preoccupied with a fear of Communist infiltration in the United States.

Though an evaluation within limits of the result-oriented school of critics can be made, an attempt to assess the criticism directed toward the judicial process is much more difficult because of the varying interpretations of the judicial process. Criticism from the process-oriented school usually manifests itself in one of two forms. The first is concerned with the judicial process per se. In essence it is a methodological disagreement with the methods and procedures used by the Supreme Court justices. These critics are not particularly interested in the outcome of any one judicial decision; rather, they are concerned with *how* that decision came about. They often take issue with the decision-making process of the judges, the number of cases examined, and even the craftsmanship put into the Court's opinions.

The second type of criticism which falls within the process-oriented school involves attacks on the judicial process or the Court as an institution, but these are for the most part predicated on decisional differences. The motivation is result-oriented, but the criticism itself is process-oriented.

It is reasonable to say that the goal of the methodological process-oriented critics is a more refined and better judicial process. The other group of process-oriented critics is primarily concerned with rectifying a decision or series of decisions, and ultimately hopes to weaken the role of the Supreme Court in order to promote its own political ideology via a competitive political institution.

To summarize, there are two areas in which criticism of the court is found wanting, and hence, subject to counter-attack. Result-oriented criticism, predicated on extreme emotionalism or irrationalism without analysis of decisions as such, precludes informed understanding of the case and does not stand the test of reasoned appeal. Process-oriented criticism also leaves much to be desired when it is not primarily concerned with sophisticating the judicial process, but rather with changing it in order to rectify a decision repugnant to the critic's ideology.

Charles Horsky has noted that "It is our responsibility...to distinguish between dissent, even vigorous dissent, and acts of hoodlumism which would warp and ultimately destroy our legal heritage."[14] Granted that this statement sounds rather harsh. Still it points up the destructive character of attacks based upon a concern with judicial results, and not upon a preferred reasoned analysis of the case as a whole.

THE CLIMATE FOR CONTROVERSY

Chief Justice Warren's opinion in *Brown v. Board of Education* constitutes a good place to begin analyzing focal points of criticism. The School Segregation cases aroused a furor. Typical of the South's reaction was Senator Harry Byrd's (D. Va.) reference to Warren as "the modern Thaddeus Stevens, now cloaked in the robes of the Chief Justice of the United States Supreme Court."[15] May 17, 1954, became known as "Black Monday" to the Court's Southern opponents.

This assault on the Court was confined almost exclusively to the South, and consisted more in political articulation than anything else. Though a great number of Court-curbing bills were introduced in Congress, not one of them was seriously considered, and the judicial process continued to function as usual.

The attack thus was ineffective because the School Segregation decisions did not materially affect anyone outside the confines of the South. It was not long, however, until the Southerners joined forces with the residual conservative groups to form a loose anti-Court coalition. The rallying point was a new trend of decisions on national security. The Warren Court — fulfilling what many liberals regard as the true function of the judiciary, the protection of individual rights against governmental encroachment — handed down a series of opinions intended as protection for citizens whose actions were regarded popularly as perhaps endangering national security. This series was highlighted by what has come to be known as "Red Monday," June 17, 1957, when the Court's majority handed down the *Watkins, Yates, Sweezy,* and *Service* decisions.[16] Each was interpreted as affronting internal security by freeing alleged "Communist conspirators," thereby giving aid and comfort to the enemy. "Red Monday" proved not an isolated event, for subsequent decisions continued to uphold the rights of individuals against energetic governmental prosecutions. The attacking conservatives made little if any analysis of these decisions. It was enough for the conservatives that suspected Communists were being freed by the Supreme Court.

COALITION EFFECTIVE

This coalition of Southern Democrats and, for the most part, conservative Republicans, formed the backbone of the groups which took the Court to task. They were especially active during 1957 and 1958. In the opinion of many, calm settled over the controversial area in 1959 with several decisions which tended to clarify and/or modify (depending upon interpretation) some of the Court's earlier controversial opinions. For example, by a 5-4 vote, the Court upheld a contempt conviction of a college professor by the name of Barenblatt who refused to answer questions posed by the House Un-American Activities Committee concerning his membership in the Communist Party.[17] This case supposedly modified the *Watkins* decision. In another case, *Uphaus v. Wyman,*[18] the Court allegedly withdrew from its position in the controversial *Sweezy* decision by upholding the contempt conviction of a minister who refused to release the names of suspected Communists who had attended a pacifist conference during a summer camp session.

In the two years following, decisions suggested a more conservative trend on behalf of the Court. The impact of the majority opinion in *Slochower v. Board of Education*[19] (in which the Court reversed the dismissal of a college professor because he had invoked the Fifth Amendment) was supposedly modified by the Court's position in *Nelson and Globe v. Los Angeles.*[20] Even more consoling to the conservatives should have been the Court's decisions in *Braden v. United States* and *Wilkinson v. United States.*[21] Here the majority confirmed the contempt citations of two persons called to testify before the Un-

American Activities Committee solely because of their criticism of the committee's action. Finally, the Court's upholding of the convictions of spy Rudolph Abel and admitted ex-Communist Junius Scales took away much of the anti-Court bloc's basis for criticism. [22]

In addition to a seemingly moderate approach adopted by the Court from 1959 on, the personnel of Congress changed. Such articulate conservatives as Senators Jenner (R. Ind.), Bricker (R. Ohio), and Knowland (R. Calif.) were no longer present to fan the fires of criticism, and in their absence the Southern senators were becoming less adamant.

A number of incidents, however, suggest that the Court controversy persisted. The late 1950's and early 1960's witnessed the rise of numerous conservative interest groups preoccupied with the problem of national security and super-sensitive to the Court's so-called "pro-Communist" trend of decisions. The moderate to conservative tone to the Court's opinions in these years appears to have had little if any impact on the conservatives of the extreme right.

ANTI-INTEGRATION REKINDLED

The irrational and frustrated bursts of criticism from such groups were fortified by a rekindling of the fires of anti-integration. Passive resistance parades in the South from 1959 to 1964, coupled with Negro student sit-ins, persuaded the more politically articulate of the South of a need for new defensive measures. Their battle against the Court was further intensified by the emergence of a new active civil rights movement under the auspices of CORE, the Congress on Racial Equality. CORE seized the initiative from the NAACP by instituting a number of pre-announced "Freedom Rides" in order to publicize the continuing discriminatory practices in the South. Consequently Southern politicians saw no choice but to continue harangues against the civil rights decisions. This situation was further invigorated not only by CORE, but by a number of companion organizations such as the Southern Christian Leadership Conference, and the Student Non-Violent Coordinating Committee.

On March 26, 1962, the Supreme Court rendered a landmark decision — long-awaited — in *Baker v. Carr*, a controversial apportionment case in which the metro-urban forces in the country attempted to effectuate a reversal of the Court's hands-off attitude set forth in *Colegrove v. Green.*[23] Justice Brennan, speaking for the majority and reversing the *Colegrove* philosophy, stated that the apportionment of legislative districts was no longer a political question which precluded the Court from hearing the case. *Baker v. Carr* threatened the very foundation upon which much of the conservative power in this country is based. A new wave of criticism was set in motion. Senator Richard Russell (D. Ga.) looked upon *Baker v. Carr* as "another major assault on our Constitutional system."[24] He further noted that "If the people really value their freedom, they will demand that the Congress curtail and limit the jurisdiction being exercised by this group (the Court) before it is too late."[25]

Within six weeks of that decision, Senator James Eastland (D. Miss.) charged — during a Senate debate on the administration's literacy test bill — that Chief Justice Earl Warren "decides for the Communists" whenever the issue is clearly between them and the security of the United States.[26] Eastland then proceeded to "rate" the justices according to their voting record in cases in which Communists were involved. No effort was made to analyze the cases as such; Eastland's only criterion was whether a justice voted for or against a Communist defendant. Eastland's tactics, reminiscent of the fierce battle which ensued in 1957 and 1958, may have been a late gust of the wind of battle. At any rate they served as a reminder that controversy had not completely subsided over the Warren Court.

2. CONGRESSIONAL CRITICISM

As the most important source of Court criticism, Congress has served the twofold function of generating and channeling attacks on the Court. The legislature is a rich reservoir of original criticism, and a conduit for the discontent of interest groups as well. Consequently it has become an excellent point of departure for analysis of judicial criticism.

The general criticism which legislators have directed toward the Court has been predicated for the most part on a "discordant social philosophy," i.e., an ideological dissent to the claimed liberal trend of judicial decisions. In addition, many Congressmen have been concerned about a number of decisions which supposedly have prevented the legislature from the free exercise of its functions. These problems are in addition to the seemingly perpetual intra-governmental struggle for power between Congress and the Court.

Criticism from the Congressional sector has been loud and frequent. Yet at the same time, if measured by legislative results, the anti-Court campaign has been a failure. Only one of approximately 200 bills has ever been enacted into law.

The School Segregation cases have been pinpointed as the inception of the current attacks on the Court. The wave of discontent following Warren's opinion in *Brown v. Board of Education*[1] still lingers in several of the hard-core Southern states. The Southern attack on the judiciary over the issue of integration in and of itself never gained sufficient momentum to pose a major threat to the High Bench, but the loose-knit coalition of segregation forces and a conservative anti-Communist movement proved to be a different story. The combination provided a firm base for challenge to the philosophy promulgated by the Court during the latter part of 1950. Although anti-Communism became the primary rallying point, there remained a strain of pro-segregationism just below the surface. Indeed, many of the attacks would begin with condemnation of an allegedly pro-Communist decision, and move subtly yet surely into the area of states' rights and segregation.

Since 1954, when the barrage of criticism began, approximately 200 bills on the over-all issue were introduced into Congress.[2] Generally speaking, these were attempts either to rectify a particular decision or to change in some measure an aspect of the judicial process. Since more than 150 or 80 per cent of these were submitted by Southern senators or representatives, it is small wonder that a continuous fibre of anti-integration feeling was visible in the criticism.

In terms of the "discordant social philosophy" dominating Congressional criticism of the Court, not only have many ideological frustrations been released, but from a more political standpoint, taking issue with the so-called "radical opinions" provides excellent fodder for newspaper headlines. It is not unreasonable to believe that much of the loud dissent from Congress has been directed toward the constituents back home, especially when the protests have concerned the trend of civil rights decisions.

Since *Brown v. Board of Education* seems to constitute the base upon which the recent attacks on the Court began, this would seem to be the logical place to begin an examination of the criticism. Warren's opinion in the School Segregation cases (as represented by *Brown v. Board of Education*) was regarded as a departure from the "Southern way of life." As such it was seized upon by politicians — often the same politicians — for two different purposes: first it became a weapon to defend what they regarded as a legitimate, moral way of life against encroachment, and second, it also helped to strengthen positions of political power by generating more judicial criticism for purposes of "home consumption." Undoubtedly most politicians were motivated by both these purposes, which are by no means mutually exclusive.

From 1954 through 1961, fifty-five bills have been submitted in Congress in an attempt to slow down the eroding away of segregation. All but two of these were introduced by Southerners. The two Northern mavericks were Representative Usher Burdick (R. N.Dak.) and Representative Katheryn St. George (R. N.Y.), both staunch conservatives. The wave of criticism was aroused, not by an isolated bill, but by a controversial political document known as the Southern Manifesto, a joint resolution signed by one hundred and one congressmen from eleven Southern states.[3] In essence, it was a declaration of "Constitutional principles" by Southern Congressmen, criticizing the Supreme Court for its ruling in the School Segregation cases. Submitted by former Senator Walter George (D. Ga.) in the upper house and by Representative Howard Smith (D. Va.) in the lower house on March 12, 1956, the declaration took the Court to task for rendering such an "unwarranted decision."[4] It noted that the members of the Court were substituting their own "personal, political, and social ideas for the established law of the land." And in view of this "exercise of naked power" the ninety-seven Democratic and four Republican signatories pledged themselves to use all legal means to bring about a reversal.

MANIFESTO IS MASKED

Although actually designed to defend and perpetuate the separation of the races in the South, the Manifesto was masked in terms of states' rights. It stated that the School Segregation cases "climaxed a trend in the federal judiciary undertaking to legislate, in derogation of the authority of Congress, and to encroach upon the reserved rights of the States and the People."[5] For the most part the states' rights plea was used, not because of virtue inherent in the doctrine, but because it afforded a slogan behind which the practice of segregation could be maintained.

The Southern Manifesto was submitted when the emotional impact from the School Segregation cases was still being felt. Whether it was primarily intended to sway votes politically or traceable to well-intended ideological differences, there were many who felt that the Manifesto was far from being based upon sound logic. Alexander Bickel has noted that it was "pregnant with the suggestion, tenable only academically or by force but not in law, that there exists a Constitution distinct from the one the Supreme Court expounds."[6]

Throughout the mid-fifties, as the race problem continued to play a large role in Court decisions, the South began envisioning itself in the role of a "whipping boy." With each new decision that upheld Negro rights, this conviction on the part of the South intensified until it might be said to have become almost a persecution complex. In 1957, after the Court had found for a Negro defendant in a criminal case, a lower court judge noted that "The opinion is the voice of the Supreme Court, but the hand is the hand of the NAACP."[7] Representative James Davis (D. Ga.) voiced the kind of psychological disturbance from which the South was suffering in describing his own reaction to *Fikes v. Alabama*, the case in dispute.[8] "In the sacrifice of the South on the

altar of the Supreme Court's psychological and sociological om-
niscience, the *Fikes* case is but another handful of salt to rub into our
wounds."[9]

More adamant critics attacked the *Brown* case purely from a funda-
mentalist standpoint. Representative J.B. Williams (D. Miss.) delivered
a speech before the Defenders of State Sovereignty and Individual
Freedom in 1957, in which he analyzed the sociological impact resulting from the Warren opinion. Williams stressed the fact that the
Brown decision would destroy the purity of the races and "pervert
moral premises."[10] "Once mongrelized," he said, "we can never re-
establish purity of race." This philosophy has been used also by the
White Citizens' Councils to rationalize their disagreement with the
segregation decisions.

The most popular mode of attack did not fall within such a funda-
mentalist category. Rather, it was directed toward the Court's exercise
of power. Representative James Davis (D. Ga.) provided a typical
illustration of this when in a speech before the Tennessee Federation
of Constitutional Government he referred to the Supreme Court's
usurpation of power — "a usurpation which amounts to tyranny,"[11]
The terms, "usurpation" and "tyranny," were probably used continu-
ally by this class of critics of the Court.

Southern Congressmen were not content with casting verbal epi-
thets. Most of the bills then introduced sought to rectify not merely
the holding in *Brown v. Board of Education,* but rather the whole trend
toward integration.

The most common form of these bills called for a Constitutional
amendment reserving control over public education to the states. Resolutions along this line were introduced by Representatives Boggs
(D. La.), Poff (R. Va.), Rains (D. Ala.), Seldon (D. Ala.), and Roberts
(D. Ala.).[12] In the Senate, Herman Talmadge (D. Ga.) submitted a bill
to the same effect.[13] These resolutions were still being presented as
late as 1961.

USE OF "SEPARATE BUT EQUAL"

Another popular method of rectifying the School Segregation decisions was by legislative fiat ruling that "separate but equal," as promulgated in *Plessy v. Ferguson,*[14] satisfied the requirements of the
Fourteenth Amendment. Senator Robertson's (D. Va.) 1956 resolution
declared that the requirements of the Fourteenth Amendment were
met through the operation of schools for different races which are separate but equal.[15] Representatives McMillan (D. S.C.), Brown (D. Ga.),

and Grant (D. Ala.) submitted similar proposals in the House of Representatives.[16] In a related attempt to nullify the Court's integration trend, Representative J. B. Williams (D. Miss), as early as 1954, proposed a Constitutional Amendment which provided that no state law shall be held to conflict with the Constitution by reason of the fact that it required segregation in public schools if the facilities were substantially equal.[17]

Southern Congressmen also attempted to exclude from the Court's appellate jurisdiction any legislative provision pertaining to the operation of the public school system for any reason other than the substantial inequality of physical facilities.[18] Several such bills were introduced as late as 1961,[19] as well as numerous others whose authors hoped to transcend the area of public education. Generally they proposed Constitutional Amendments to preclude interference with what they regarded as the exclusive power of the states to regulate "health, morals, education, marriage, and good order in the State."[20]

Two other proposed Constitutional Amendments, one in 1956 and one as late as 1961, sought the same broad goal. The 1956 proposal was conceived by Representative Carl Vinson (D. Ga.), Chairman of the House Armed Services Committee and a powerful figure in the House. It stated that the several states "shall forever have the right to manage their own internal affairs with respect to any matter not expressly forbidden by the Constitution.[21] The 1961 bill by Representative Oren Harris (D. Ark.) attempted to give citizens the right to segregate themselves voluntarily from others for any lawful purpose as provided by state law.[22] Viewed together, these two bills illustrate the persistent and stereotyped nature of the proposals from Southern critics during a six-year period.

CRITICISM NOT EFFECTIVE

Though exceptionally vocal, Southern criticism of the Supreme Court on the issue of segregation never had a substantial effect on either the Court or the public. Not one of the fifty-five bills submitted for consideration was ever enacted into law. Indeed, none was even reported out of committees so as to be considered on the floor of the House or Senate, in spite of the fact that Senator James Eastland was chairman of the Senate Judiciary Committee. The anti-Court bills may have been submitted for purposes of public dissent more than for any other reason. On the other hand, the lack of Congressional action may have been due to most of the bills being proposed by Southern Congressmen who wielded relatively little influence. Bills which did emanate from the more powerful Congressional figures, such as Representative Carl Vinson (D. Ga.) and Senator Harry Byrd (D. Va), seemed to be fabricated more from political rhetoric than from action. Whatever the reason, there is little evidence that the Court's prestige suffered outside the confines of the South. It was not until the issue of segregation was fused to the anti-Court campaign over the public offender cases that any threat to the judicial process arose.

CAMPAIGN RE-ENERGIZED

This new trend of civil liberties cases supposedly offending our national security re-energized the anti-Court campaign. Such cases were primarily those in which the rights of unpopular citizens, in particular Communists or alleged Communist sympathizers, were protected against governmental prosecution. The public offender cases involving Communism reached many more people than did the sectionalized civil rights conflict. As previously described, Southern Democrats and conservative Republicans were united in combating what they believed to be the internal threat of Communism. In the course of this combat the anti-civil rights cause was also promoted.

Illustrative of the emotional nature of the criticism during this period was a statement by Senator Strom Thurmond (D. S.C.) to the effect that "while we are thinking of tyranny in Hungary, I wish to take a few minutes to discuss tyranny in the United States; and when I say that, I mean the tyranny of the judiciary in the United States."[23] Thurmond referred to the trend of decisions pertaining to integration as well as to security cases.

An even more vivid example of irrational criticism comes from a speech made on the floor of the House by Representative Howard Smith (D. Va.). In July of 1957, the powerful chairman of the House Rules Committee stated that he could not recall a single case decided by the Warren Court which the Communists had lost.[24] Smith made no attempt whatsoever to analyze the content of the decisions to which he referred. His sole concern was with the result. Conspicuously absent was any recognition of the delicate Constitutional problem which balances the relationship of human rights with the issue of national security.

Senator James Eastland (D. Miss.), chairman of the Senate Judiciary Committee, also depends on result-analysis in his condemnation of the judiciary. The Senator favors a game of drawing box scores of the justices' voting records in order to demonstrate the pro-Communist trend of decisions. In 1958, Eastland claimed that the Warren Court as a whole was overly sympathetic to the claims of Communists,[25] and produced statistics to show the following "pro-Communist" voting percentages:

Justice	Percent	Justice	Percent
Black	100	Harlan	58
Douglas	95	Burton	46
Warren	92	Whittaker	36
Brennan	90	Clark	35
Frankfurter	77		

Even the conservative justices — Harlan, Burton, Whittaker, and Clark — came in for this attack.

The Senator from Mississippi provided another result-oriented analysis of Supreme Court voting as late as May 3, 1962.[26] This score was revealed during a Southern filibuster against a bill to outlaw literacy tests for voting. In addition to blanket criticism of the Court, Eastland specifically focused his attack on Chief Justice Warren.[27]

Eastland's criticism has not been limited to the box score approach. His attacks have been frequent and varied. At times they have focused attention on the Court as a super-legislature rewriting the laws enacted by Congress, as a barrier which has reduced the sovereign states to a position of "mere vassalage," and as an institution which has "emasculated" the power of the Presidency.[28] But the recurrent theme is the Court's pro-Communist rulings. "In decision after decision, the Court has given aid and comfort to the Communist conspiracy. . . ."[29]

The Senate and House have numerous other spokesmen who enjoy riding the tide of anti-communism. On May 5, 1959, Representative Dale Alford (D. Ark.) rose in the House and delivered the following attack on the Court:

> The greatest emergency which confronts our country today is not the Soviet or Red China or Berlin crisis or inflation; it is the destruction of the Constitution of the United States of America by oath-breaking usurpers who are now members of the Supreme Court.[30]

Alford at this time proposed to reconstitute the Supreme Court so that the Senate rather than the President would take over the process of selecting future justices.

In a similiar vein, Representative Mendel Rivers (D. S.C.) has characterized the Supreme Court as a "greater threat to this Union than the entire confines of Soviet Russia."[31] Representative Overton Brooks (D. La.) presented the problem in more detail.[32] He told members of the House that Moscow first intended to establish a Communist Negro Republic in the "black belt" of the South. Later, when this failed, Brooks said that the Communists shifted their attention to the Supreme Court. The Representative from Louisiana attempted to substantiate his theory by pointing to the fact that the justices are now relying on sociological and psychological evidence in the formulation of their opinions. According to Brooks, many of the sociologists were either Communists or members of Communist front organizations.[33]

The effort here seems to be to prove "guilt-by-association." Reasonable analysis of the substance of decisions is lacking as usual. Instead, subtle phrasing often manages to cloak the Court in an aura of pro-Communist sympathy, as in this comment from former Senator William Jenner (R. Ind.) in 1958.

> Reasonable men may err. If the Court had erred only once or twice in these decisions involving the greatest threat to human freedom, reasonable men could find excuses for it. But what shall we say for this parade of decisions that came down from our highest bench on Red Monday after Red Monday.[34]

Association of judicial decisions with the cause of Communism, combined with failure to discuss the merits of any of the cases in point, may be found in a speech by Representative Donald Jackson (R. Calif.), who said: "Nothing in recent years has given greater impetus or encouragement to the resurgence of the American Communist apparatus than have recent decisions of the American Supreme Court."[35]

On another occasion he spoke of deploring "a tendency to permit [the Constitution's] living phrases to be distorted and twisted to meet the immediate needs of those whose dedicated purpose is to destroy it and replace it with the Constitution of the Soviet Union."[36] This statement was preceded by the remark that the Court's recent decisions "have lent aid, comfort and assistance to our national enemies."[37]

AIDS IN REVERSALS

The anti-Communist support given by this type of attack can be drawn upon by dissident Congressmen in their attempts to reverse a number of the Court's more controversial decisions. Witness Representative Scherer's (R. Ohio) declaration that unless "these decisions can be nullified by action of the Congress, there will be a resurgence of Communist activity in the United States that will not only make your hair curl, but your stomach turn."[38]

Certain criticism has on occasion showed some insight into the problems involved. Representative Wint Smith (R. Kan.) in 1958 took issue with the Court's holdings in several cases involving national security, and though he emphasized the end result, he attempted to substantiate his view by arguing that the Court in balancing equities was simply "blind to the reality of our time."[39] Representative William C. Cramer (D. Fla.) pointed out that the Court in dealing with cases of Communist subversion fails to recognize the practical problems and workings of Congress in its attempt to legislate on the problem.[40] Valid or not, at least these arguments are predicated upon issues which could affect the outcome of a particular decision.

Southern Democrats and conservative Republicans attempt to rebuke the Court often through the adoption of critical and restrictive resolutions. A bill proposed by Representative Scherer (R. Ohio) in 1961 was designed to reverse the supposed civil rights trend by ruling that certain individuals who refused to testify before a federal agency with respect to subversive activities would be ineligible for any right, privilege or benefit under any law of the United States.[41] Most of the bills were not nearly this extreme.

QUALIFICATIONS BECOME AN ISSUE

The qualifications of prospective justices, and the manner in which they were to be selected have been among the more popular subjects utilized by conservative Congressmen to chastise the Court. Since 1954, at least fifty-four pieces of such legislation have been proposed with respect to these problems but none ever got out of committee. Fifty-one of these were initiated by Southerners — the same individuals who had been most vocal in condemnation of recent judicial decisions. This suggests strongly that the proposals were instigated to discredit the Court because of political dissent rather than to enhance the caliber of justices. Had the bills been successful, the category of persons most eligible to act as justices would have been drawn from a conservative mold, not unlike the legislators who were attempting to set the qualifications.

Senators Talmadge (D. Ga.) and Ellender (D. La.) attempted to establish a requirement that all future appointees of the Supreme Court have at least five years judicial experience in a lower federal court or in the highest tribunal of a state.[42] Numerous other bills were submitted based on the same condition. Since the highest appellate courts of the states are known for being conservatively oriented[43] (though this is less true with respect to the lower federal courts), appointments from this area would more than likely be politically and socially conservative. Representative Abernethy (D. Miss.) called for a like measure in his bill. In addition, Abernethy would have made an

appointee ineligible if five years prior to the appointment the prospective juror had served as a congressman, head of an executive department, Vice President of the United States, the director of certain
governmental agencies, or member of certain commissions.[44]

Senator Russell Long (D. La.) and Representative Don Wheeler
(D. Ga.) were not satisfied with the five-year requirement suggested
by Talmadge and Ellender. They demanded that at least one half of
the persons appointed to the office of associate justice have at least six
years experience in a lower federal court or the courts of the several
states.[45] Representative Robert Casey (D. Tex.) wanted at least eight
years' experience,[46] while Representatives Winstead and Smith, and
Senator John Stennis, all of Mississippi, held out for ten.[47]

Another group of Southern congressmen wanted to spell out the
requirements more specifically. In addition to the ten years of judicial
experience, a justice had to be born a citizen, thirty-five years of age,
a resident of the United States for fourteen years, and a graduate of a
law school accredited by the American Bar Association.[48] Since even a
group as tightly knit as the conservative Southern bloc could not agree
on whether they should require five, six, eight or ten years of experience, it appears that these men were more concerned with opposing
the "usurping" justices currently gracing the High Bench than changing the qualifications.

In addition to judicial experience, the length of a justice's term of
office also provided an area ripe for discontent with the Court. One
group of Congressmen wanted to limit a term to ten years.[49] Still another felt a four-year term was more than enough.[50] Senators Eastland (D. Miss.) and Johnston (D. S.C.), realizing that this might mean
too large a turnover, provided for reappointment with the advice and
consent of the Senate.[51] Senator Long (D. La.) proposed a similar
bill but with a twelve-year term.[52]

Numerous other proposals tended indirectly to take the Court
to task. Senator Johnston (D. S.C.) called for a Constitutional Amendment to the effect that judges could hold office only during a period of
good behavior,[53] suggesting that certain judges were not currently
satisfying this condition. Representative Overton Brooks (D. La.) called
for the whole Supreme Court to be reconstituted so that the justices
could be drawn from the highest appellate tribunals of one-third of the
several states.[54] He argued that the process of judicial selection should
be taken out of the hands of the Attorney General since the present
system placed the states at a disadvantage.[55] Representative Usher
Burdick (R. N.Dak.) seized upon an age-old suggestion of the American
Bar Association that the ABA provide the President with names of

seventy-five lawyers to assist him in making appointments whenever a vacancy occurred on the Court.[56] This suggestion was welcomed by the Southerners, since the ABA has always been dominated by conservatives.[57] Another Congressman, George Grant (D. Ala.), called for approval by the House of Representatives before justices could be appointed to the Supreme Court.[58] Representative James Davis (D. Ga.) called for the establishment of a commission on constitutional law.[59] This was to be composed of seven to fifteen of the nation's eminent lawyers, past presidents of the ABA, former state chief justices, and outstanding appellate jurists.[60] Finally, Representative Robert Sikes (D. Fla.) proposed a means of weakening critically the role of the judiciary. Sikes called for a Constitutional Amendment making the Senate a court of final appellate jurisdiction to review all Supreme Court decisions affecting the powers reserved to the states or the people.[61]

ATTACKS POLITICALLY MOTIVATED

These attacks on the composition of the Supreme Court, whether or not valid in their own content, appear to have been politically motivated, as were two bills, proposed by Congressmen Abbitt and Tuck of Virginia, to require unanimous consent among the justices in order to invalidate any provision of a state constitution or statute.[62] Since many of the recent controversial decisions had been in fact far from unanimous, such a bill would have further promoted conservative efforts to check the "judicial activism" of the Court. Francis Walter (D. Pa.), a powerful conservative, would have required the concurrence of not less than five justices in the granting of writs of *certiorari*.[63] All three of these proposals died in committee.

A number of other bills would have had the effect of limiting the power of the Court. Representative Huddleston (D. Ala.) submitted a resolution which provided that the courts of the United States and of the several states would not be bound by any decision of the Supreme Court which conflicted with legal principles found in a prior decision and which were clearly based upon non-legal considerations.[64] This was undoubtedly a rebuke to the Court for failing to follow the segregation line set forth in *Plessy v. Ferguson* (separate but equal), and for incorporating sociological and psychological evidence in making a determination in the School Segregation cases.

Carl Vinson (D. Ga.), the influential Chairman of the House Armed Services Committee, submitted an even less camouflaged attack on the Court's holding in *Brown v. Board of Education.*[65] The 1956 Vinson bill provided that no decision of the Supreme Court which had remained in effect for fifty years or more would be subject to review unless authorized by an Act of Congress. Since *Plessy v. Ferguson* (1896) would not have satisfied this fifty-year requirement in 1954 at the time of the *Brown* decision, Vinson specifically provided that any decision rendered by the Supreme Court since January 1, 1954, when arriving at the fifty-year terminal point, would be null and void. Congressman Robert Sikes (D. Fla.) called for a Constitutional Amendment to prevent the Court from modifying or changing any prior decision construing the Constitution or Acts of Congress.[66] One wonders if Representative Sikes realized that passage of this amendment would have preserved the Court's ruling in *Brown v. Board of Education* for all time. Finally, a proposal by Congressman Whitener (D. N.C.) would have prevented the United States from filing a brief *amicus curiae* or appearing in any other fashion in a civil action in federal courts except as a real party in interest.[67] This was obviously an attempt to prevent the government from throwing its moral and legal weight behind the efforts to stamp out segregation, as it had in *Brown v. Board of Education*. None of the above bills reached the floor of the House.

Less subtle than these political maneuverings were some of the attacks directed toward the decision-making processes. Representative William Cramer (R. Fla.) told the House of Representatives that the opinions of the various justices were so vague as to offer Congress no guideposts,[68] a line of reasoning adopted by numerous critics.[69] The difficulty that several lower courts have had interpreting the intention of many majority opinions suggests that there is much truth to this.

TYPES OF EVIDENCE CRITICIZED

Controversy revolves also around the types of evidence used by the justices in their attempts to arrive at a just decision, especially with respect to the use of "non-legal" factors such as sociological and psychological evidence. Representative Wright Patman (D. Tex.) professed that it was no longer clear what factors were being used.[70] He claimed that the Court was resorting to "unrecognized and non-authoritative textbooks, law review articles, and other writings of propaganda artists and lobbyists." Patman did not say, however, what criteria *should* be used. It is difficult to conceive how legal issues involving the economy and civil rights can be resolved without considering economic, sociological, and psychological evidence. It would appear that this issue had been settled nearly fifty years before with the incorporation of the Brandeis brief as an effective and useful evidentiary tool.

Still, the problem of using so-called "non-legal" factors was ex-

ploited to the limit by the segregation critics who condemned the
Court for its emphasis upon Gunnar Myrdal's *An American Dilemma*[71]
in the School Segregation cases. Senator Eastland in an article entitled
"An Alien's Ideology Is Not the Law of Our Republic," referred to
Myrdal as the "Swedish Carpetbagger." He chastised the Court for
predicating its opinions on the teachings of "pro-Communist agitators
and pepole who are part and parcel of the Red Conspiracy. . . ."[72] Representative Brooks levied a similar attack, spelling out in more detail
that Theodore Brameld, a contributor to *An American Dilemma,* had
invoked the Fifth Amendment frequently while testifying before the
House Un-American Activities Committee.[73]

A further line of criticism pertains to the use of law clerks, and was
initiated in an article by a former clerk to Justice Robert Jackson —
William H. Rehnquist. This article noted, among other things, that the
"political cast of the clerks as a group was to the left of either the nation
or the Court."[74] In addition, he claimed that this philosophy included
an "extreme solicitude for the claims of Communists and other criminal
defendants, expansion of federal power at the expense of State power
. .and great sympathy toward any governmental regulation of business" on behalf of some of the liberal clerks he knew.[75] The article
prompted Senator John Stennis (D. Miss.) to call for an investigation
of the law clerk system to determine the extent that these clerks influence the opinions of the justices.[76] Few would doubt that the burden
carried by Supreme Court justices is great, and perhaps there is a
very real problem here since many justices of necessity rely heavily on
their clerks. The distressing feature of these indirect criticisms of the
Court is that they were presented at a time when anti-Court fever was
at its height. And under these circumstances, it is not difficult to believe
that at least the Stennis article was a deliberate political maneuver
to chastise the Court.

ATTACKS ON PERSONALITIES

A final manifestation of criticism within the "discordant social
philosophy" sphere deals with attacks upon judicial personalities. This
type of criticism took on numerous forms, ranging from criticism of a
justice's attitude on the nature of law to an emotional attempt to draw
a relationship between a justice and the Communist conspiracy. Representative Noah Mason (R. Ill.) charged that Justice Frankfurter had no
respect for laws enacted by Congress or the states. He said that Frankfurter always favored a strong federal government and ignored the
states and individuals.[77] The Illinois Republican cited no evidence to
substantiate his opinions.

Even more vitriolic was an attack on Chief Justice Warren by Representative James Utt (R. Calif.).[78] Utt prefaced his remarks by stating that he was not going to engage in an attack upon the Supreme Court as an institution; he was only interested in chastising those members of the Court who had used social philosophies as predicates upon which to base their decisions. The Congressman then proceeded to examine aspects of the Chief Justice's personality which he found to be offensive, including an analysis of Warren's relationship with former Vice President Nixon and columnist Earl Mazo. The best that can be said for this criticism is that it falls short of the bitter statement by Senator Harry Byrd (D. Va.) portraying Chief Justice Warren as a present-day "Thaddeus Stevens."[79]

The broadest Congressional attack upon the judicial personality was delivered by Representative Wint Smith (R. Kan.) in 1957.[80] He examined a number of the justices individually, giving in each instance a basis for his disapproval. Black was criticized for his lack of judicial experience; Warren's role as Chief Justice was attacked as being nothing more than an expedient political appointment. In addition, Warren had advocated "socialized medicine" in California and "this is the first step Communists use in organizing a totalitarian state." Warren also was accused of helping Harry Bridges defeat the right-to-work bill in California in 1944. Justice Brennan also felt Smith's fire. Brennan supposedly had insufficient tenure on the bench "and in any event was no Medina." Finally, Justice Frankfurter, who often voted with the liberal bloc, was taken to task for his pre-Court liberal ideas.

An indirect and subtle attack was used by Representative Coleman (D. Ala.), who called attention to articles in Communist newspapers praising certain Supreme Court decisions. A related item found in a British Communist newspaper praised Justice Black for his decision in one of the more controversial cases. Coleman, having made the connection between Communism and Black, then appealed for Congress to take action "before the Court destroys this nation."[81]

Perhaps even more surprising have been attacks on the Court's personnel as a whole. Without singling out any individual, Clare Hoffman (R. Mich.) called for impeachment of the justices because their decisions were resulting in the virtual overthrow of the government "through fallacious reasoning, rendering decisions which made Constitutional provisions void."[82] Congressmen Mason (R. Ill.) and Andrews (D. Ala.) followed up Hoffman's attack by advising that they were seeking the services of "one of the best lawyers in America to prepare an impeachment resolution against all members of the High Bench."[83]

Both of these threats of impeachment came after the "Red Monday" decisions.

DECISIONAL OBSTRUCTION

Quantitatively less but equal in importance to criticism springing from discordant social philosophy are attitudes toward judicial decisions preventing Congress from exercising its authority fully and freely. When the Court has stepped in and advised the legislature to move with more caution and precision in certain areas, numerous Congressmen have become irate and instituted procedures designed to eliminate future judicial obstruction.

The best known instance of this is the 1957-58 controversy over the Jenner-Butler bill.[84] The original Jenner bill contained five separate provisions, each of which was a response to a particular judicial decision. The bill would have prevented the Supreme Court from assuming appellate jurisdiction (1) over cases involving the admission to practice law in the several states — overriding the *Konigsberg* and *Schware* cases; (2) over the activities of Congress or Congressional investigating committees with respect to proceedings involving witnesses charged with contempt of Congress — overruling the *Watkins* case; (3) over the power of the executive branch to dismiss governmental employees under a loyalty-security program — overruling the *Cole, Peters,* and *Service* cases; (4) over the acts and regulations of states, the general purpose of which was to control subversive activities — overruling the *Nelson* case; and (5) over the actions of educational institutions concerning subversive activities in its teaching body — overruling the *Slochower* case. Given the present composition of the Supreme Court, Senator Jenner (R. Ind.) was not satisfied that the results of these cases would ever be rectified by judicial decree. Hence, he chose simply to prevent the Court from ruling in these areas thereafter. This would have meant that the issues in the Jenner bill would finally be determined either in the highest court of a state or one of the lower federal courts of appeal. With fifty different state jurisdictions and eleven federal circuits including the District of Columbia, the Jenner bill could have resulted in sixty-one different interpretations of any of the five named Constitutional questions.

Senator Butler (R. Md.) amended the Jenner bill, leaving intact only the provision dealing with admission to the Bar of the several states. Instead of eliminating the Court's appellate jurisdiction over certain areas, the Jenner-Butler bill simply attempted to rectify the holdings in certain cases. It attempted to express Congressional intent on such problems as the meaning of "advocacy" and "organize"

(*Yates* case), on the scope of the term "pertinency" and who would decide the issue of pertinency in Congressional investigations (*Watkins*), and on expressing a Congressional desire that the states not be precluded from enforcing their respective statutes unless there is a direct and positive conflict between the state and federal law which cannot be reconciled (*Nelson*).

The Jenner-Butler bill was tabled by a 49-41 vote. However, the anti-Court resolution is a measure of the Congress's determination to eliminate whatever check is being exerted upon its powers.

WATKINS MOST OFFENSIVE

The *Watkins* case, in which the Court handed down a decision limiting the power of the House Un-American Activities Committee, constituted the most injurious thorn in the side of Congress. This committee had been the subject of numerous liberal attacks because of its claimed "brow-beating" tactics. When the Court not only admonished the committee verbally, but also commanded it to provide more safeguards for its witnesses, this was simply too much for the security-minded legislators to take. Senator Jenner (R. Ind.) commented that the *Watkins* decision had dealt the investigating committee a "body-blow by making it possible for witnesses to stop an investigation in its tracks."[85] *Watkins*, he felt, had multiplied the danger of Constitutional imbalance "by severely crippling, if not wholly smashing, the Congressional power to investigate."[86] Charles Wolverton (R. N.J.) echoed Jenner's feelings, emphasizing the fact that in the future Congress would be greatly handicapped in the effectiveness of its investigations.[87] Whatever the limitations placed by the Court upon Congress in the *Watkins* decision, a number of Congressmen viewed this case as an impediment to the free exercise of legislative function, and as such, *Watkins* was an obstruction which had to be removed; hence, the Jenner bill. The fight was not entirely abandoned though the *Barenblatt* decision,[88] combined with a number of political factors alluded to earlier, mitigated the demand to curb the Court over this issue. As late as 1961, Representative Kathryn St. George (R. N.Y.) proposed a bill incorporating the provisions of the original Jenner bill in hopes of resolving the issue more favorably to Congress.[89] The resolution was never acted upon.

INTRA-GOVERNMENTAL CONFLICT

Among the little-mentioned aspects of the Congressional anti-Court campaign is the issue of "intra-governmental conflict." Generally speaking, this is simply a struggle for power among the various branches of government. The Court competes with Congress and the President; the President wages his campaign against the Court and Congress; and Congress is caught in the midst of a power struggle not only between the Court and the President, but also between its respective houses. Generally, the immediate cause is a particular governmental policy which each institution is promoting. But in addition, there is a struggle for power *per se*, for only by continuously solidifying its own power vis-a-vis other governmental agencies can each branch be assured of an opportunity to make itself felt on future issues.

Because it is almost always accompanied by an ideological problem, "intra-governmental conflict" is not readily conspicuous. Hence, it is necessary to pierce the veil of political criticism to see if there is not something more than a mere "discordant social philosophy." This is not always an easy task.

The most frequent evidence of intra-governmental conflict is signified by the cry of "judicial encroachment." Illustrative of this is Democratic Senator Sam Ervin's statement, "We are ruled in large measure by judicial oligarchy, ... The Court is destroying the power of the states and is encroaching on Congress and the Executive."[90] In a more irrational outburst, Representative Dale Alford (D. Ark.) told the House that "the greatest emergency which confronts our country today is not the Soviet or Red China or Berlin crisis or inflation; it is the destruction of the Constitution of the United States . . . by oath-breaking usurpers who are now members of the Supreme Court."[91] "Judicial legislation," "usurpation," " judicial activism," all of these are phrases which reveal Congressional concern over the power of the Court.

This jealous intra-governmental struggle for power is evidenced in any volume of the *Congressional Record*. Representative Donald Jackson appealed to Congress to curb the Court because it was "putting the Congress of the United States out of business."[92] Senator Eastland characterized the Court as taking unto itself powers "without any justification in statute or Constitution . . . without any reliance on recognized principles of law, without any basis whatever except its own naked thirst for power."[93] And Senator Strom Thurmond, in testifying on the Jenner bill, said that the Court "has consistently moved to expand its power, until it threatens to be the dominating power in the Government."[94] "The time has come," remarked the Senator from South Carolina, "for action by the Congress to call a halt to this unconstitutional seizure of power by the third branch of government."[95]

Congressional critics are not, however, quite so upset by the Supreme Court's checking on the activities of a competitive political branch of government. Joseph Menez has pointed out that the Court was viewed as the true guardian of the Constitution when it held that President Truman was trespassing in attempting to seize the steel mills in 1952.[96] But the moment the Congressional critics find themselves on the restricted end of a judicial decree, this constitutes an "unwarranted usurpation of power."

In fact, a peculiarity of the Court's "naked thirst for power" is that as a general rule the judiciary is extremely deferential to Congress. This has been revealed in a number of studies which have viewed the relationship of Congress and the Court from almost every standpoint.[97] Congress has a tendency to protest when it is the subject of limitation, but not if the President is held in check.

Former Senator Kenneth Keating (R. N.Y.) has made a perceptive commentary on "intra-governmental conflict." He told an audience at the University of Maryland:

> ...the controversy between Congress and the Court in recent years is an inevitable and perhaps even an intended result of the division of governmental responsibility decreed by the Constitution. It is an example of our system of checks and balances.[98]

Indeed, this "intra-governmental conflict" is harmonious with the concept of limited government which plays such a significant role in the American political system.

CONCLUSION

It appears then that Congress has attacked the Supreme Court primarily because the conservatives in the legislature have been ideologically offended by the claimed liberal trend of judicial decisions. These Congressmen have concentrated in vain for the most part on proposing remedial legislation in hopes of reversing the Court's decisions. Indeed, it is significant that only seven percent of some two hundred odd bills ever reached the floor of the House or Senate, most of these submitted by Congressmen who did not wield a great deal of influence. When proposals were offered by the more powerful conservatives, they were restricted to public condemnations of the judiciary. Thus from a Court-curbing standpoint, the legislative process was more attuned to an exercise in rhetoric than determined political action.

In another vein, many Congressmen were moved to condemn the Court because of its supposed power threat to Congress. This was simply an aspect of the intra-governmental struggle for power which necessarily results when power is divided among several branches of government. Closely related to this issue was the problem of "decisional obstruction." Several of the Court's decrees had been interpreted as hindering Congress in the full and free exercise of its legislative function. In particular, the *Watkins* decision supposedly handcuffed the House Un-American Activities Committee in its investigation of the "Communist conspiracy." This resulted in an energetic, yet futile, attempt by the conservatives in Congress to preclude the Court from reviewing the activities of the House Un-American Activities Committee.

On the whole, the efforts of the conservatives in Congress to mount an effective campaign against the Supreme Court were unsuccessful. This was particularly true when the issue of segregation constituted the only rallying point for the critics of the Court. The creation of a loose-knit bloc in Congress bound together by a segregation-anti-Communist philosophy did increase the threat to the judiciary, but proved to be more vocal than effective.

The failure of the anti-Court campaign in Congress can probably be attributed to several factors. In the first place, there appeared to be a reluctance on the part of the more influential conservatives in Congress to act as catalysts in getting the proposed bills out of committee and ready for action. Secondly, the Court's critics as a whole appear to be satisfied with a campaign of rhetoric as opposed to one of political action. This is further demonstrated in the next chapter in an examination of the Congressional response to particular decisions handed down by the Court.

3. CONGRESSIONAL RESPONSE TO JUDICIAL DECISIONS

The bitter criticism emanating from the South following the decision in the School Segregation cases has been the subject of much debate. But this was only the beginning in a series of attacks directed toward the Warren Court. The aftermath of the School Segregation period was perhaps even more important than the earlier conflict, for by now the critics of the High Bench were coupling the issue of segregation with the internal threat of Communism, thereby broadening their political base and providing the twofold nucleus from which most of the Congressional criticism develops.

An insight into the onslaught on the Court is afforded by examining in greater detail the Congressional response to some of the controversial decisions. In investigating the attempts of a number of congressmen to remedy the problems allegedly posed by such decisions, it is apparent that in certain instances Congress and the Court worked hand in hand to solve problems. At the same time it is evident that Congress frequently attempted to weaken the judicial process in order to prevent the Court from checking legislative activities.

Any detailed investigation of Congressional response should begin on "Red Monday," the summer day in 1957 when the Court handed down four decisions reversing governmental prosecutions which involved Communists or alleged Communist sympathizers.[1] The first case to arouse Congressional anger was *Yates v. United States.*[2] Yates was one of fourteen Communists convicted after being indicted under sections two and three of the Smith Act which make it a crime for anyone knowingly to teach or advocate or organize a group which teaches or advocates the overthrow of any government of the United States by force or violence.[3] Conviction was affirmed by a federal court of appeals,[4] but reversed by the Supreme Court for five of the petitioners, including Yates.

Congress was disturbed not only by the fact that the Communists were now free, but primarily by the construction which the Court's "principal" opinion gave to the term "organize." Justice Harlan, speaking for the Court, interpreted "organize" according to its "natural and obvious import," i.e., the initial establishment of a party. Since the Communist Party had been dissolved in 1941 and re-established in 1945, it was the latter date to which the term "organize" applied. The importance of this interpretation rests in the fact that there is a three-year statute of limitations which applies to all federal crimes. Since Yates and four of his fellows had not been indicted until 1951, the three years had passed and the petitioners were no longer subject to prosecution. In addition to construing narrowly the "organization" clause, the Court defined "advocacy" as "advocacy directed at promoting unlawful action." This was to be distinguished from "advocacy in the abstract." Under the advocacy clause, the Court found the over-all evidence insufficient to support a conviction of five of the petitioners. There was adequate evidence, however, to sustain the conviction of the other nine petitioners.

AIMED AT REVERSAL

A number of bills were introduced into Congress in an effort to reverse the decision, most of them directed toward rectifying the construction placed on "organize" and "advocacy." A certain portion of the Jenner bill was so-directed in 1958,[5] as well as a subsequent bill submitted by Senator Keating in 1959.[6] The most comprehensive resolution aimed at rectification in the *Yates* case was offered by Representative Francis Walter in 1961.[7] The resolution defined "organize" to include the recruiting of new members, and the forming of new or the expansion of existing subversive units. This was intended to eliminate such narrow construction of the "organization" clause as given by the Court in the *Yates* case, thereby preventing Communist access to the three-year statute of limitations.

The Walter bill defined the term "advocacy" as supposedly to eliminate the distinction between intentional advocation at inciting unlawful action and "advocacy in the abstract," making advocacy in and of itself a crime. Such a construction might well have been held unconstitutional had it been enacted into law, for it appears to be repugnant to the First Amendment provision for free speech, of which Congress "shall make no law abridging." It should be noted, however, that Congress must be granted its prerogative to enact such legislation with an eye to the fact that it runs the risk of offending the Constitution. At any rate, no bill defining the terms "advocacy" or "organize" has passed both legislative chambers.

The abortive attempt to change the Court's construction of the term "organize" points up one aspect of interacting legislative-judicial functions in the political process. Justice Harlan stipulated that it was not entirely clear just what Congress had intended with respect to the term, and therefore, the Court had no choice but to apply the Constitutional construction which dictates that terms be interpreted in their strictest sense. It remained for Congress to spell out that intent which is precisely what the legislature attempted to do with its definition of "organize." Hence much of the general criticism directed by the liberals toward Congress for attempting to negate an aspect of a Court decision was unwarranted as Congress was simply fulfilling one of its proper functions in clarifying its intention for future judicial consideration. One version of the Walter bill passed the House in 1959,[8] but subsequent proposals died in committee.

In *Sweezy v. New Hampshire*,[9] the state legislature had authorized the attorney general of New Hampshire to conduct a one-man investigation into the activities of suspected subversive persons within the state. He subpoenaed Paul Sweezy, who, though testifying on most matters and denying his own membership in the Communist party, refused to comment on those subjects which he felt were not pertinent to the inquiry. In particular, the petitioner refused to discuss his knowledge of the Progressive Party in New Hampshire or of persons with whom he was acquainted in that organization. In addition, Sweezy refused to discuss a class lecture given to students in 1954, an article on pacifism that he had co-authored, and certain questions pertaining to his opinions and beliefs. The petitioner was convicted of contempt, but this conviction was reversed by the Supreme Court on the grounds that the inquiry invaded his right to academic freedom and political expression. The Court held also that the state legislature had not provided an adequate basis for controlling the investigation. Though the decision of the Court was directed toward a *state* legislature, Congress, caught up in its furor over "Red Monday," felt that the *Sweezy* decision constituted an unwarranted "usurpation" of legislative power by the judiciary.

An attempt to remedy this decision was made in several of the anti-Court curbing bills. A general provision in the Jenner bill would have precluded the Supreme Court from assuming jurisdiction over cases involving state statutes, the general purpose of which was to control subversive activities.[10]

In *Watkins v. United States*,[11] the defendant answered all questions with respect to his own activities and relationship to the Communist Party; however, he refused to answer questions concerning persons who had since quit the Party, and that he knew in the past to have been members. Watkins was convicted of contempt. Upon appeal to the Supreme Court, the case was reversed and remanded to the lower court for further consideration.

RIGHT VIOLATED

The decision to reverse rested upon the failure of the House Un-American Activities Committee to show Watkins why the questions he refused to answer were pertinent. This failure violated the defendant's right to due process of law. Though the holding of the case rested on this narrow ground, Chief Justice Warren's opinion was fraught with dicta which tended to mislead the critics of the Court.[12] With respect to the charter of the House Un-American Activities Committee, Warren commented that it was "difficult to imagine a less explicit authorizing resolution."[13]

Warren's pursuit of the question of legislative power to investigate provoked a heated controversy within the legislative chambers. Congressmen were incensed for a number of reasons. This third "Red Monday" decision appeared to be another in a series of systematic blows to the national security program, while of equal importance was the blow the Court had struck to the prestige of Congress. Warren took the legislature to task for its zealous and oft-times reckless investigating procedures, and noted that "There is no congressional power to expose for the sake of exposure."[14] Even more damaging to the ego of Congress was the Chief Justice's statement that "Investigations conducted solely for the personal aggrandizement of the investigators or 'to punish' those investigated are indefensible."[15] The security-conscious members of Congress had already been placed on the defensive by liberal attacks condemning a number of Congressional investigators as "publicity seekers." The legitimate sanction Warren's opinion gave this condemnation must have been too much for the conservatives, whose reaction was immediate and startling.

As in the *Sweezy* case, primary legislative response to *Watkins* revealed itself in the Jenner bill. The general provision dealing with the *Watkins* decision prevented the Supreme Court from reviewing "any function or practice of...any committee or sub-committee of the United

States Congress, or any action or proceeding against a witness charged with contempt of Congress."[16]

SECURITY IS CONCERN

Beyond the issue of "intra-governmental conflict," the *Watkins* decision provoked anti-Court sentiment because of its end result — it permitted a "security risk" to go free after having been found in contempt of Congress. The critics of the Court were not satisfied with manifesting a general dissent. They felt a need to eliminate temporarily, or at least erode the barrier to their program of national security by the role of the judiciary as a political check on legislative action. Had the Jenner bill been successful, it might have set a precedent by which Congress could have stopped the Court from reviewing its actions in any number of cases. This could have resulted in the development of a power vortex in Congress.

The *Watkins* case exemplifies that criticism of a judicial decision may be cast in several molds. It evidenced discontent because of "decisional obstruction," "intra-governmental conflict," and "discordant social philosophy." Foremost among these, however, was the result-oriented fundamental fear that the decision would jeopardize internal security.

Of the four cases handed down on "Red Monday," the last — really three cases in one — was *Service v. Dulles*.[17] Less controversial than the others, it nevertheless had the misfortune of being rendered on "Red Monday." Service, a Foreign Service Officer, had been subjected to a barrage of security checks during his term of employment with the government. Each time he had been cleared. In 1951, during the third review of his fifth clearance, the Loyalty Review Board decided that Service now constituted a security risk and recommended his dismissal to the Secretary of State. Service was thereupon notified of his dismissal by the Department of State. The determination was made "solely as the result of the finding of the Loyalty Review Board and as a result of [the Secretary's] review of the opinion of the Board."[18] Service appealed his case all the way to the Supreme Court, which held that the Secretary of State (Acheson at this time) had not complied with the State Department's own regulations for the discharge of a federal employee in security cases. The holding of this case was not particularly startling in and of itself, but it was the last in a series of three cases involving the issue of loyalty-security.

The first of these, *Peters v. Hobby*,[19] involved a Yale professor of medicine employed as a part-time consultant to the U.S. Public Health Service, a non-sensitive position in the government. Upon the review of his second clearance, it was recommended that Peters be dismissed for loyalty reasons. When Peters appealed his discharge, the Supreme Court upheld his contention on the grounds that the Loyalty Review Board did not have the statutory right to review the case. The second in the series, *Cole v. Young*,[20] also involved a non-sensitive position. Cole, a food inspector for the Food and Drug Administration, was summarily dismissed when he refused to answer charges that he had been associating with Communists and attending the meetings of organizations on the Attorney General's list. The Court, in reversing the decision of the Health, Education, and Welfare Department, held that employees in non-sensitive positions did not fall under the Summary Suspension Act of 1950.

DECISION ON NARROW GROUND

Each of the three cases was decided on a narrow procedural ground. The combined results, however, gave rise to a rebuttable presumption that the Court had handed down a firm and significant ruling on the loyalty-security program. Climaxed by the *Service* case, this series of decisions provided still another ground for the Court's security-conscious critics.

Again the Jenner bill served as the key to rectification of the trend of decisions. The Jenner bill would have eliminated all such loyalty-security cases from the Court's appellate jurisdiction.[21] Prior to the Jenner bill, numerous resolutions had been introduced in an effort to rectify *Cole v. Young*.[22] The closest Congress came to reversing the "systematic trend of decisions" was when the legislature almost passed S. 1411.[23] As conceived by the administration, this bill would have refined some of the procedural problems inherent in the loyalty-security program. The bill as passed by the House (298-46), however, went much further. It extended the Summary Suspension Act to include all governmental jobs including those classified as non-sensitive.[24] The bill eventually died when the Conference Committee failed to reach an accord in time for Congress to act upon it.

The critics of the Court's position on the loyalty-security issue did not give up their fight. The House again submitted a bill in 1959, but failed to get it out of committee.[25] And in the Senate, a resolution was offered which would have permitted the head of any governmental agency absolute discretion in discharging an employee who was thought to constitute a security risk.[26] As late as 1961, Representative Francis Walter continued the anti-Court battle by once again offering a bill which included placing non-sensitive employees within the purview of the Summary Suspension Act.[27]

Two years after *Service v. Dulles*, in *Greene v. McElroy*,[28] an aeronautical engineer was denied security clearance by the Navy to do work involving classified data for a private concern. The denial was effected under the government's industrial security program. Accused of associating with Communists, Greene was never apprised of the source of the charges nor was he given an opportunity to confront his accusers. Since the firm engaged only in classified work, Greene had to be discharged. The majority of Supreme Court justices sustained the petitioner's claim to employment, but the Court carefully avoided predicating its decision on the ground that the procedures utilized under the industrial security program violated the Fifth or Sixth Amendments. Chief Justice Warren simply stated that "in the absence of explicit authorization from either the President or Congress the respondents were not empowered to deprive Greene of his job in a proceeding in which he was not afforded the safeguards of confrontation and cross-examination."[29]

SECURITY PREOCCUPATION

Congressional response to the *Greene* case again points up the grave preoccupation of some Congressmen over national security. Here was a case in which an individual was denied the prerequisites of a fair hearing. Yet when the Court found such a procedure not authorized by Congress or the President, the critics of the Court responded with a set of bills designed to shore-up the security program, regardless of individual rights. Typical of this was Francis Walter's proposed legislation, which would have permitted the Defense Department to make security risk findings without confrontation of witnesses and cross-examination.[30] Though Walter's bill passed the House, its several companion bills in the Senate died in committee.[31]

The issue dealing with industrial security was finally resolved when President Eisenhower issued an executive order codifying much of the philosophy inherent in the majority opinion in the *Greene* case.[32] Confrontation of witnesses and the right to cross-examination became the general rule rather than a neglected exception. This compromise seemed to placate the conservative critics who had been unable to reverse the *Greene* decision via legislation. The importance of the *Greene* case lies in the fact that it reveals the great schism in social philosophy between the security-minded legislators and a moderately liberal Court.

The problem of passports also generated a conflict between security-minded legislators and the Court. *Kent v. Dulles* was the background for this series of attacks.[33] The Court upheld the petitioner's contention that the Secretary of State could not deny Kent a passport simply because the State Department found him to be a Communist. Once again the Court skirted the Constitutional issue and decided the case on the ground that Congress had not given the Secretary of State the right to deny a passport "because of beliefs or associations."[34] This decision resulted in the granting of visas to persons heretofore considered security risks. Exemplifying the concern this aroused among the security-minded conservatives, Senator Jenner argued that the trend of judicial decisions respecting passports resulted in "Communist conspirators... being dispatched abroad on treasonous errands."[35]

PASSPORT CONTROVERSY SPREADS

The passport controversy was not limited to Congress. Eisenhower, in urging Congress to pass an administration-sponsored bill, said that "Each day and week that passes without [this bill] exposes us to great danger."[36] The Presidential bill would have left it to the discretion of the Secretary of State to deny a passport to anyone whose activities aided Communism during the ten-year period prior to the application.[37] In spite of the President's message of urgency to Congress, the bill never got out of committee in the Senate. In 1959, the House passed a passport resolution, but it was stymied by lack of Senate action.[38] The 1959 House bill was a compromise, incorporating the philosophy demanded by the Court's critics and at the same time providing some procedural safeguards for the applicant.[39] In 1960, another effort was made to change the state of affairs with respect to the *Kent* ruling. A passport provision was incorporated in a general internal security bill in the Senate, but the bill never reached the floor.

Another case involving national security had been decided two weeks before "Red Monday" and generated considerable ill feeling toward the Supreme Court. Indeed, *Jencks v. United States*[40] acted as a preview of future Court action. Jencks was a labor leader who had filed a non-Communist affidavit with the National Labor Relations Board. The government questioned the validity of this affidavit and prosecuted Jencks for swearing falsely that he was not a member of the Communist Party. Two witnesses for the government testified that Jencks had been an active member of the Party. Since the witnesses had previously given statements of which they could not recall the content to the FBI, the petitioner's counsel requested that the statements be examined in order to test their validity. The trial judge denied counsel's request, the issue was appealed to the Supreme Court, and counsel's request to examine the controversial reports was sustained.

CONFUSION IS RESULT

The Court's opinion in the *Jencks* case caused considerable confusion for a number of reasons. In the first place, the initial request was for the trial judge to examine the controversial reports. Justice Brennan, however, widened the scope of this issue by stating that counsel for the defense should be the one to examine the reports. He reasoned that only the defense counsel is equipped adequately to determine whether the statements might be used to impeach the testimony of the witnesses. Justices Burton and Harlan, though concurring in the end result, would first have required the trial judge to scrutinize the material in order to "seal off" matters not relevant to the issue. In this way, only that portion of the material pertaining to the issue would be disclosed to counsel for the defense, and materials pertaining to national security would be safeguarded. Under Brennan's interpretation, the government would have to choose between releasing the documents in full, thereby possibly revealing classified information, or dismissing the case.

The sweeping generalizations inherent in Brennan's majority opinion gave rise both to misunderstanding and ill-feeling. The conservatives' response was certainly not discouraged by the biting dissent of Justice Clark who laid a foundation for the critical response of Congress:

> Unless the Congress changes the rule announced by the Court today, those intelligence agencies of our government engaged in law enforcement may as well close up shop, for the Court has opened their files to the criminal and thus afforded him a Roman holiday for rummaging through confidential information as well as vital national secrets.[41]

The expected barrage began with Representative Usher Burdick's statement that the *Jencks* decision had the same effect as putting the "FBI out of business...This decision encourages crimes. It encourages the underworld, and it is a blow to law enforcement."[42] Senator Potter (R. Mich.) commented that the Court had turned "governmental records into a free peepshow for alien powers."[43] And Representative Wint Smith (R. Kan.), continuing to perpetuate the conservative internal security line of reasoning, said that the "Warren Court has now thrown its protective cloak around fellow travelers and Communists. The Court is simply blind to the realities of our times."[44] Numerous bills were introduced in order to clarify the *Jencks* decision, and their tone on the whole, was not overly emotional. The bills were directed not at giving the Supreme Court a "slap-on-the-wrist," but attempted to strike a balance between the issues of national security and individual rights.

APPROACH IS CONSTRUCTIVE

The most important of the bills was presented by Senator O'Mahoney.[45] The Wyoming Democrat provided a focal point for thoughtful, yet firm clarification of the *Jencks* decision. Much of the lack of public condemnation of the Court at this time may be attributed to the fact that O'Mahoney insisted on a constructive approach to the problem as opposed to an emotional Court-curbing atmosphere. And since he was chairman of the subcommittee to which the bill was assigned, O'Mahoney was largely successful in his efforts.[46]

Meeting the demands of the competing groups was not easy. The bill in its final form attempted to capture the spirit enunciated in the *Jencks* case. A court, on the motion of defense counsel and after a witness had testified on direct examination, could order the government to produce certain reports for inspection. The Court would first examine the reports to determine what portions were relevant to the testimony in issue, and then permit the delivery of that relevant portion to be used for purposes of cross-examination. If the government failed to comply with the directive, then the testimony of the witness in controversy would be stricken from the record.

Numerous side issues tended to block immediate passage of the bill. Should oral reports be included? Could material from a pre-trial discovery be used? These problems and more were hurdles which O'Mahoney finally vaulted successfully after drafting five versions of this delicate piece of legislation. The final bill as passed by the Conference Committee embodied more of the concurring opinions of Burton and Harlan than it did the principal opinion of Brennan. At any rate, the essential philosophy of the *Jencks* case had been codified with a minimum of anti-Court criticism. The fact that Congress felt the need to enact any legislation indicated some concern over the Court's decision, but in the long run, the passage of the bill demonstrated that conflicts between the Court and Congress need not be entangled in a maze of emotion.

The critical response by Congress to certain decisions of the Supreme Court has not been limited to cases involving the federal government. Judicial decisions adversely affecting the states have also served as targets for attack on the Court.

CONGRESS AS A MEDIUM

The sympathies of congressmen are in many instances in accord with the states, so that Congress can act as a medium for articulating state grievances — especially those involving the fight against Communism.

Foremost among the decisions affecting state programs for national and state security was *Pennsylvania v. Nelson*.[47] Nelson, an acknowledged Communist, was tried and convicted under the Pennsylvania Sedition Act, a statute used by the state to prosecute Communists. Upon appeal, his conviction was upheld by the Pennsylvania Superior Court, but reversed by the State Supreme Court. The United States Supreme Court sustained the State High Court's verdict, which was predicated upon rather narrow grounds. In essence, the majority opinion affirmed that in the absence of an expressed intent to the contrary, the scheme of federal regulation with respect to sedition against the United States was such that it evidenced congressional intent to occupy the field.[48] Note that the *Nelson* case dealt only with the question of a state's right to prosecute cases of sedition against the United States government, it did not proscribe state activity with respect to sedition against the state government.[49] The pre-emption issue, however, was interpreted by numerous critics as entirely preventing the states from acting regardless of jurisdiction. Hence, an erroneous reading of the *Nelson* decision led to a significant misunderstanding of the scope of the Court's opinion.

Congressional reaction was vigorous. The critics of the Court now had a new weapon with which to attack the judiciary — states' rights. Security-minded congressmen would no longer have to belabor their political differences with the liberals over the question of national security alone, for compounding this with states' rights would make a far more compelling argument. Typical of this style of attack was Representative Noah Mason's (R. Ill.) statement that it "is only a question of time before all power and all sovereignty residing in the States to enact and enforce laws will be taken over by the federal government."[50] Representative James Davis (D. Ga.) noted that "it is apparent that the ultimate intention of the Supreme Court is to abolish every vestige of States' rights."[51] Davis went on to state that the Court's decision in *Nelson* was a "brazen and irresponsible attack on the sovereignty of all of the States."[52] The Court, noted Davis, "has dedicated itself to the complete destruction of the States."[53] Representative Andrews (D. Ala.), in his condemnation of the Court, stressed the testimony of a former president of the American Bar Association who had noted that 98 percent of the "good" lawyers of America had no respect for the legal ability of the present members of the Court.[54] No definition was offered of "good" lawyers.

LEGALITIES OVERLOOKED

As voiced, Congressional response failed to deal with the legal aspects of the *Nelson* decision. Most of the critics were preoccupied with defending states' rights. Actually, all that was needed to rectify the Court's decision was an expression of legislative intent with respect to enforcing acts of sedition against the United States. There remained, of course, the question of the wisdom of having numerous states compete with the FBI and the federal government in prosecuting suspected security risks.

Approximately seventy bills were introduced in Congress to rectify the Court's position, and all but four died in committee. The major legislative controversy centered around H.R. 3,[55] an especially general piece of legislation which was proposed by Representative Howard Smith (D. Va.), the influential Chairman of the House Rules Committee. The language relevant to the *Nelson* decision in H.R. 3, as well as most other bills, may be summarized in two sections:

> Prohibits any Act of Congress from being construed as indicating an intent on the part of Congress to occupy the field in which such Act operates to the exclusion of all state laws on the same subject matter, unless expressly stated, or in direct and positive conflict.

> Except as specifically provided by federal statute, any federal law providing for criminal penalties for acts of subversion or sedition against the federal government or a state government, shall not prevent enforcement in state courts, of state statutes prescribing criminal penalties for such offenses.

The first provision deals with the problem of preemption in general (there was concern over the problem of preemption in other areas such as labor relations); the second deals with the issue of sedition per se. Though there were individuals who questioned the wisdom of enforcement of the national security program at any level other than the national, few argued that Congress did not have the right to determine this.

The implications of the general provision generated some grave problems. As the minority report on H.R. 3 noted, this bill could have taken the nation back to the time of the Articles of Confederation. [With a scope so broad it could have affected materially the body of laws which dealt with labor relations, inter-state carriers, and integration, among others.] Even the late Francis Walter, who always had aligned himself with the security-conscious critics of the Court, indicated that he was not quite sure just what the general provision entailed, and thus opposed it.[56]

Attempts to enact H.R. 3 and its companion bills in the Senate — S. 337 and S. 654 — into law have been thwarted continuously,[57] but the legislative struggle has been a long and hard one. As late as 1961, Representative Howard Smith (D.Va.) still was offering H.R. 3 as a potential statute to mitigate the Court's holding in the *Nelson* case.

SENATE BARRIERS LOOM

The year 1958 climaxed the preemption battle. H.R. 3 had easily passed the House,[58] but the barriers in the Senate proved greater. Two bills required consideration. S. 337 dealt with the general provision on preemption, while the more important one — S. 654 — was restricted to an effort to reinstate state authority in prosecuting sedition cases, i.e., rectifying *Pennsylvania v. Nelson*. A bitter fight ensued in the Senate over S. 654, which was finally defeated through a procedural tactic, 41-40. Though H.R. 3 again passed the House in 1959, no action was taken in the Senate.

Much of the concern which accompanied the legislative struggle over the preemption bills from 1957 through 1959 can be attributed to the ideological dissent from security-conscious Congressmen. A witness to this may be found in Representative Donald Jackson's (R. Calif.) statement that "I am frank to admit that my support of H.R. 3 is, in major part, emotional."[59] The fervor surrounding the issue was displayed in the vigorous floor debates which raged between the Jenners, Thurmonds, and Eastlands on one hand, and the Clarks, Carrolls, and Churches on the other. At times it appeared that the contest was not over the passage of a piece of legislation, but rather over the censure of the Court. During the 1959 debate, Representative Rogers (D. Colo.) stated that the enactment of H.R. 3 "is an attempt to tell the Supreme Court of the United States how to conduct its business."[60] And Representative O'Hara (D. Ill.) stated that "H.R. 3 is the rock. The Supreme Court is the target."[61] Though H.R. 3 was never enacted into law, it certainly provided an opportunity for numerous attacks on the Court — direct and indirect.

Besides the *Nelson* case, several others provoked ill feeling among the states' rights advocates. Three in particular gave rise to attacks upon the Court. Two of these cases, *Schware v. New Mexico Board of Bar Examiners*[62] and *Konigsberg v. State Bar of California*,[63] involved state restrictions on admission to the practice of law. Both cases fall under the same general category but are quite distinct in their respective import. Schware had been denied admission to the Bar in New Mexico for several reasons, including prior arrests, the use of aliases, and because he had been an admitted member of the Communist Party between 1932 and 1940.[64] The last ground was the primary basis for exclusion. The Board of Examiners held that this constituted bad moral character. The Supreme Court reversed this decision, stating such a finding could not have constituted bad moral character so as to exclude the petitioner from the practice of law. Since there was no rational connection to be made here to Schware's fitness to practice law, the ruling of the Board of Examiners contravened the clauses of the Fourteenth Amendment on due process and equal protection of laws.

REFUSAL TO CERTIFY

In the *Konigsberg* case, the California Bar Examiners refused to certify the petitioner because he declined to answer the questions on his political beliefs. According to the Bar Examiners, the petitioner failed to satisfy the condition of "good moral character." The only evidence leading to this conclusion was the testimony by one witness that Konigsberg had attended a Communist meeting in 1941, and that the petitioner had written a newspaper article criticizing the Korean War, actions of leaders of major political parties, the influence of big business in American life, racial discrimination, and certain decisions of the U.S. Supreme Court. Justice Black, in the majority opinion, stated that writing such criticisms did not infer bad moral character. The second issue with which the Court dealt was not as clearly spelled out, but it had to do with the right of the petitioner to remain silent.

The third case which gave rise to ill feelings among the states' rights advocates also dealt with the right to remain silent under certain circumstances. *Slochower v. Board of Higher Education of New York City*[65] involved an associate professor at Brooklyn College who was summarily dismissed because he had invoked the Fifth Amendment before the Internal Security Subcommittee. His dismissal was made in accordance with a provision in the New York City Charter calling for the termination of employment under such circumstances. Upon appeal, the Court held that the exercise of an individual's Constitutional right to invoke the Fifth Amendment cannot be taken as being equivalent to a confession of guilt. Hence, the petitioner's summary dismissal upon such a ground was violative of due process.

The holdings of the Court in all three of the above mentioned cases offended the conservative philosophy of security-minded Congressmen. Each of these cases, directly or indirectly, crystallized for security-minded Congressmen the fact that the Court was "letting Communists and fellow travelers out of jail" and encroaching on the sanctity of states' rights. Representative James Davis (D. Ga.), when speaking of the *Slochower* case, asked "where is the usurpation of States' rights going to end?"[66] Representative Noah Mason (R. Ill.) traced the history of the erosion of states' rights back through the years of Franklin D. Roosevelt and up to and including the administration of Dwight Eisenhower. He attempted to show how the "New Dealers, Fair Dealers and Modern Republicans" had captured the Court as a tool by which to weaken the states.[67] The road to tyranny that "we have been traveling for the past twenty years" must end. According to Mason, this could only be brought about by curbing the Court.

JENNER BEST KNOWN

Again the proposed Jenner bill was the best-known mechanism for curbing the Court. When Senator Butler (R. Md.) attached his amendment to the Jenner bill, the only provision left standing was the one that prevented the Court from assuming jurisdiction of cases involving the admission to the practice of law. The provision placing the rules and regulations on school boards or similar educational bodies concerning subversive activities among teachers was eliminated by the Butler amendment. The Jenner-Butler bill of course was tabled by a 49-41 vote in the Senate in 1958.[68] This defeat, coupled with the Court's rendering of several moderate decisions in the field of states' rights, helped to clear the air of controversy.[69]

One very controversial case which provoked ill feeling in Congress was not related to the issue of Communism at all, but it was a criminal case dealing with the rules of criminal procedure. Congressional response to *Mallory v. United States*,[70] however, was no less than the reaction to the cases already examined. This case was decided in 1957, the same year in which a number of unpopular political offender decisions were handed down, and may have been provocative for that reason. Further substantiating this view is the fact that the *Mallory* case is really no more than an extension of a rule of procedure set forth in an earlier criminal decision, *McNabb v. United States*.[71] Although the *McNabb* decision was controversial, it never generated the degree of criticism which arose over the *Mallory* decision.

In the *Mallory* case, confusion has arisen because different aspects have been emphasized from time to time to create different impressions. The petitioner, a nineteen-year-old Negro of limited intelligence, had been arrested on a charge of rape. He was taken to a police station where he was continuously questioned for seven and a half hours, subjected to a lie detector test, and finally confessed to having committed the crime. He was convicted on the basis of this confession. The core of the legal conflict was that Mallory had not been arraigned until after his confession was obtained. In the light of ample evidence from other sources revealing the petitioner as the chief suspect, and the fact that an arraignment could have easily been effected during Mallory's detention, the Supreme Court voided the conviction on the basis that there had been an unreasonable delay in arraignment. This violated Rule 5 (a) of the Federal Rules of Criminal Procedure.[72] Since Mallory's confession had been obtained during this unnecessary delay, it was considered to be inadmissible evidence.

CONGRESSIONAL RESPONSE VARIED

The immediate vocal response from Congress was varied. Senator Strom Thurmond demanded curbing of the powers of the Court. In addition to protecting Communists, the Court "has now issued an edict which will give greater protection to such heinous criminals as rapists and murderers."[73] On the other hand, Representative Poff (R. Va), a conservative colleague of Thurmond, attempted to analyze the case from a legal standpoint. Poff took issue with the Court's holding that there had been an "unreasonable" delay in the arraignment, but his argument was neither emotional nor devoid of decisional examination.

Approximately thirty-three bills were introduced in Congress in an attempt to rectify the precedent set down in the *McNabb* case and extended in the *Mallory* decision. The respective drafts were almost identical in content and provided that confessions or other evidence shall not be deemed inadmissible solely because of a delay in arraignment unless the effect of the delay is to render the confession involuntary.[74] Only one bill passed the House;[75] the rest died in committee.

The rationale of the criticism here and of the proposed rectification, is that the Court was overemphasizing legal technicalities. Yet as Alan Barth has stated, it is precisely such technicalities that make up the backbone of a free society.[76]

Legislative apportionment is one of the more recent controversies around which criticism of the Supreme Court has centered. For years the Court had declared this to be a political question and not the proper subject of judicial determination. As Justice Frankfurter has noted, the problem of apportionment falls within the province of Congress, and the judiciary ought not to enter into the "political thicket" in order to rectify a problem beyond its competence.[77]

In 1962, the Supreme Court reconsidered the alleged Court position with respect to legislative apportionment, and came to the conclusion that the judiciary not only could, but should review the constitutionality of apportionment schemes. In the first apportionment decision, *Baker v. Carr,*[78] Justice Brennan argued that the Court had never fully embraced Frankfurter's idea that apportionment constituted a political question. While the problem of apportionment obviously had political overtones, it was not political to the extent that it constituted a non-justiciable issue. A political question, according to Brennan, was one which involved the doctrine of separation of powers, i.e., a dispute between two or more of the three branches of government. Apportionment, on the other hand, was not an issue growing out of the doctrine of separation of power; rather, it dealt with the consistency of state action as applied to the Constitution.

QUESTIONS ARE LEFT

After all of the intricacies of Brennan's opinion were stripped away, *Baker v. Carr* did one thing. It held that the federal courts could hear cases involving apportionment — nothing more. What constituted fair representation, what formulas were to be used, these and many other questions were left to be determined in subsequent cases.

The second major case in the controversy over apportionment decisions was *Gray v. Sanders.*[79] Actually the *Gray* decision dealt with a tangential issue — the constitutionality of the Georgia county-unit system as a scheme for holding primary elections. While the facts in *Gray v. Sanders* reveal some of the inequities in state apportionment, the real importance of the case flows not from the facts, but rather from the philosophy of the Court as spelled out in Justice Douglas' majority opinion. Speaking in terms of political equality, Douglas reasoned that:

> from the Declaration of Independence to Lincoln's Gettysburg Address, to the 15th, 17th, and 19th amendments, [political equality] can mean only one thing — one person, one vote.[80]

Douglas here provided a preview of how the Court would handle cases in the future. Indeed, the very next year the Court used the "one person, one vote" phrase to determine the constitutionality of Georgia's congressional districts. In *Wesberry v. Sanders*,[81] Justice Black struck down Georgia's apportionment scheme with respect to congressional districts. Instead of focusing on the Equal Protection Of Laws clause of the Fourteenth Amendment, Black chose to concentrate on Article I, Section 2, of the Constitution. Here, he reasoned, it was stipulated that members of the House of Representatives must be chosen *by the people* of the several states. Black concluded that, as nearly as is practicable, one man's vote on a congressional election must be worth as much as another's. Here the Douglas philosophy of "one person, one vote" became the criterion for fair representation in congressional elections.

While the *Wesberry* case caused a great deal of public concern, especially among conservatives, the Supreme Court was not yet finished with apportionment. Several months after the *Wesberry* case, the Court startled the rural power elite across the nation with another decision threatening the political control which rural forces held over many state legislatures. Actually, there were six separate decisions, but the prevailing philosophy may be found in the leading case — *Reynolds v. Sims*.[82] Chief Justice Earl Warren, speaking for the majority, concluded that the Equal Protection of Laws clause of the Fourteenth Amendment required that *both* houses of a state legislature had to be apportioned on the basis of population — again "one man, one vote." Warren reasoned that legislators represented not trees or acres, but people. State representatives were to be elected by voters, not by farms or cities or economic interests. In view of this, whenever a person's vote was diluted by residence in a city or an urban county, he was denied the equal protection of laws.

This series of decisions is extremely complicated. The concurring and dissenting opinions of each case are a study in themselves. The importance of these decisions, however, rests not in analysis of the merits of the various opinions, for as Chief Justice Charles Evans

Hughes said, "The Constitution is what the judges say it is." Since the philosophy of "one man, one vote" prevailed, this legal issue was largely closed. The real battle now was in the political arena, and in particular, in the hands of the rural forces whose power was threatened with erosion.

RURAL RESPONSE VIGOROUS

The response of the rural power elite to the apportionment cases was immediate and vigorous. Their strategy initially consisted of efforts to pass a constitutional amendment which would reverse the underlying philosophy of the decisons. Senator Everett Dirksen proposed such an amendment in the Senate as did Representative William McCullock (R. Ohio) in the House.[83] But time was of the essence, and the passage of a constitutional amendment might take more time than was available to the Court's critics.

The Eighty-eighth Congress met the problem head-on in August, 1964. In the House, Emmanuel Celler (D. N.Y.), chairman of the House Judiciary Committee, was favorably disposed toward the Court's philosophy and posed an immediate obstacle to the efforts to override the decisions. In spite of this, Representative William Tuck (D. Va.) submitted a bill designed to stop the federal courts from assuming jurisdiction in cases involving state legislative apportionment.[84] The bill was sent to the Judiciary Committee for consideration. In an attempt to kill the bill, Celler didn't even call a hearing on it. Led by chairman Howard W. Smith (D. Va.), the House Rules Committee, in a rarely used procedural tactic, finally reported the Tuck bill to the floor over Celler's strenuous objections. After rejecting several amendments designed to weaken the bill, the House passed it by a vote of 218-175.[85]

In the upper House, Dirksen still hoped to remedy the problem by a constitutional amendment. Having initially decided against the statutory avenue chosen by the House, Dirksen proposed a two-to-four year "stay" of the federal court orders.[86] This would have provided Congress with the time required for the passage of a constitutional amendment. The Dirksen bill was favorably reported out of the Senate Judiciary Committee, but ran into trouble on the floor of the Senate. A compromise bill was finally accepted by Dirksen and Majority Leader Mike Mansfield, and offered as an amendment to the pending Foreign Aid Appropriations bill. The Dirksen-Mansfield amendment immediately provoked a filibuster by a handful of liberal senators who favored the Court's apportionment decisions. When an attempt to cut off the filibuster by cloture failed, Mansfield conceded defeat. Ultimately the Senate passed a mild resolution suggesting that the federal courts permit the state legislatures up to six months to comply with the various court decrees.[87] The conservative forces had lost the first round.

When the Eighty-ninth Congress convened in January of 1965, efforts were renewed to reverse the "one man, one vote" philosophy. This time concentration was on the passage of a Constitutional Amendment. By March, 1965, 21 states had petitioned Congress to call a Constitutional convention for the purpose of reversing the Court's apportionment decisions (34 states are needed for such a convention). While the possibility of such a convention appears rather remote, this state pressure gave needed support to the Dirksen amendment which was re-introduced at the beginning of the Eighty-ninth Congress. The efforts of the Illinois Republican proved to be of no avail, however, for his amendment again failed to pass the Senate.

A HIGHLIGHT OF RESPONSE

The Court's handling of the School Prayer case was a highlight of congressional response to judicial decisions, since it probably generated more immediate emotional feeling than any case since *Brown v. Board of Education.* The decision involved a non-denominational prayer drafted by the New York Board of Regents for oral recitation by each classroom in the New York State system. No child was compelled to recite the prayer. Students could be excused from the classroom upon the request of the parents. Five parents sued to enjoin the recitation of the prayer on the grounds that it violated the First and Fourteenth Amendments to the Constitution.[88] The Supreme Court agreed with this contention. Justice Black, in delivering a 6-1 opinion, stated that the New York Board of Regents, by using its public school system to encourage recitation of a non-denominational prayer, had adopted a practice wholly inconsistent with the establishment clause of the First Amendment.

The Congressional response was explosive. Republicans and Democrats alike took the floor in Congress to condemn the decision. Representative Frank Becker (R. N.Y.) called the decision "the most tragic in the history of the United States."[89] Senator Herman Talmadge (D. Ga.) said that it was an "outrageous edict which has numbed the conscience and shocked the highest sensibilities of the nation."[90] Representative Mendel Rivers (D. S.C.) commented that the Court had "now officially stated its disbelief in God Almighty," and noted that the Court was "legislating" with "one eye on the Kremlin and the other on the National Association for the Advancement of Colored People."[91] Representative Thomas Abernethy (D. Miss.) echoed Rivers' statement and proclaimed that the decision would please no one but

a few atheists and Communists.[92] Representative Francis Walter
(D. Pa.) remarked that the decision was in line with others handed
down by the Court recently, and that it was Congress' own fault that
nothing had been done about it.[93] Senator Robert Byrd (D. W. Va.)
continued in the vein of Representative Walter's criticism, stating that
"somebody is tampering with America's soul. I leave to you who that
somebody is."[94] Representative George Andrews (D. Ala.) stated that
"They put Negroes in the schools and now they've driven God out."[95]

Proposed amendments designated to override the decision were
immediately introduced into Congress. In the House, Representative
Taylor (D. N.C.) drew up a proposal to legalize prayer and Bible reading in public schools.[96] And in the Senate, J. Glenn Beall (R. Md.) and
John Stennis (D. Miss.) and Willis Robertson (D. Va.) all took similar
action.[97]

The emotional quality of the criticism in this case is probably as
great, if not greater, than that which accompanied the School Segregation decisions. As Anthony Lewis of the *New York Times* has phrased
it, much of the criticism was "abuse" and not a rational discussion of
the Court's reasoning. The greater hazard to supporters of the School
Prayer decision case than of the School Segregation decisions lies in
the emotionally generated attempt to attribute an anti-God belief to
anyone who defends the Court's action.

RESPONSES VARY

It is evident that congressional response to the decisions handed
down by the Court in recent years has not been all of a kind.

Not all of it by any means has been negative. Indeed, the liberal
forces in Congress have rallied to the judiciary's defense on numerous
occasions. Senator Wayne Morse (D. Ore.), former Dean of Oregon
Law School, has frequently clashed with the Court's critics on the floor
of the Senate. The Senator from Oregon seemed to delight in explain-
ing away the box score statistics which Senator James O. Eastland
(D. Miss.) so frequently used in his analyses of the Supreme Court.[98]

In addition to Morse, several other liberals in the Senate consist-
ently have defended the Court against conservative attacks. The late
Senator Richard Neuberger (D. Ore.), following a discussion of the
Jencks case, praised the work of Chief Justice Warren and noted that
the appointment of Warren had been one of President Eisenhower's
major attainments while in the White House.[99] Senators Javits (R. N.Y.),
Clark (D. Pa.), Hennings (D. Mo.), Langer (R. N.Dak.), Douglas
(D. Ill.), and Proxmire (D. Wis.) all assumed roles similar to those of
Morse and Neuberger. Senators Javits and Clark in particular cham-

pioned the defense of the Court. Clark, in expressing liberal opposition to the Jenner-Butler bill, argued that the proposed Court-curbing legislation created a "totalitarian tendency" in this country.[100] In echoing Clark's sentiments, Senator Javits reasoned that the bill would pose a grave threat to the independence of the judiciary — a fundamental tenet of democratic philosophy. In noting that most criticism is healthy, Javits argued that many of the attacks on the Court were based upon a misconception of the nature of the Constitution and the functions of the Court.[101] These examples, though few in number, exemplify the tone of the liberal forces as they defended the Court against conservative criticism.

4. RESPONSE OF THE INTEREST-GROUP CRITICS

Interest groups, private organizations, and individuals have always played an important role in the American political system, and consequently have been operative also in the attacks on the Supreme Court. This large cluster of critics objects to the decisions of the Court almost entirely from an ideological standpoint, and its attacks are result-oriented, with little if any attention devoted to problems of the judicial process.

Interest-group critics promote their particular causes by direct pressure on Congress through lobbyists and sympathetic legislative representatives. They also attempt to mobilize sections of the electorate in the hope that members will exert pressure upon their respective congressmen. Above all, interest-groups can issue a clarion call to the public with this end in view by arousing not only the public, but Congress as well. Indeed, most of the judicial criticism from interest-groups has this latter quality.

The interest group critics are so varied and numerous that it is difficult to categorize these critics for analytical purposes. There are, however, two groupings which are basic. The first consists of the emerging conservative organizations often referred to as the radical right. More and more articulate of late, these groups constitute a major source, and include not only such patriotic groups as the John Birch Society, but also ultra-conservative newspapers and columnists which have been especially energetic in their criticism of the Warren Court.

The second category covers such traditional conservative associations as the Veterans of Foreign Wars and the American Legion.

Though not as vocal as the radical right, they have-been heard significantly in the anti-Court campaign. Activity of these traditional interest
groups is not always open to public scrutiny. Indeed, their effectiveness is at times owing to influence exerted on a personal-relationship
basis. The scope of this study, however, includes only the overt examples of judicial criticism.[1]

THE RADICAL RIGHT

Regardless of whether or not it is true as claimed that a new wave
of conservatism is sweeping the nation, it is a fact that the "far right"
has become more articulate in recent years, and is responsible for much
of the verbal abuse directed toward the Supreme Court.

The John Birch Society has been outstanding in this articulation.
Founded by Robert Welch in 1958, the Birch Society calls itself a
patriotic organization, the sole purpose of which is fighting the "Communist menace." "We are fighting Communists— *nobody* else,"
exclaims Welch in his *Blue Book*.[2] The size of the Birch Society's membership is not published, but several sources have estimated it to be
around 90,000,[3] with chapters in all fifty states and the District of
Columbia. In addition to local unit meetings and an occasional speech-
making tour by Welch, the society publishes a pamphlet entitled
American Opinion. In 1961, this bulletin had a paid circulation of over
14,000, and was supposedly growing at a rate of 1,000 per month. By
1965, circulation had risen to slightly over 26,000. Occasionally, several
of the more popular articles from *American Opinion* are combined
into the *American Opinion Dollar Reprint Series*. One item in this
series, "One Dozen Candles," is a symposium on anti-Communism
including an article by Rosalie Gordon entitled "Nine Men Against
America." Articulate spokesmen and a small but militant following
have placed the Birch Society among the more formidable critics of
the Court.

Welch follows the line of result-oriented criticism when he says
that the "tidal wave" of pro-Communist decisions began with the
School Segregation cases, which were followed by a number of pro-
Communist and anti-states' rights decisions. He argues that local and
regional governments are the greatest bastions against a Communist
take-over, and hence, any anti-states' rights holding would constitute
an erosion of the American defense against Communism. It is Welch's
position that Communism and socialism are almost one and the same,
and that "the whole Supreme Court is a nest of socialists and even
worse."[4] The Birch Society has proposed to solve the problem by
attacking the Court's personnel.

CAMPAIGN TO IMPEACH WARREN

Though Roosevelt, Truman, and Eisenhower have led the country "down the road to socialism," the Birch Society views the Chief Justice as the power behind the "whole socialist machine." Thus in January, 1961, the Birch Society instituted a campaign to impeach Earl Warren. Members of the Society were urged to write their Congressmen in order that the Warren Court "could be stopped from its transformation of our Constitutional Republic into a mobocracy, and from giving aid and comfort at every turn to our Communist enemies."[5]   If this was not stopped, they were advised that the United States would go the way of Poland and China and Cuba. Automobile stickers reading "Impeach Earl Warren" were made available. A campaign was started of writing letters to newspapers. Members were urged to discuss the issue with friends, get resolutions passed in other organizations whenever practical, and form Impeach Earl Warren committees. It is even reported that during a football game in Cleveland, an airplane flew over the stadium with a trailer upon which was written "Impeach Earl Warren."

The Birch Society evidently does not expect the impeachment attempt to be successful, but rather, that the movement will dramatize and crystallize "the whole basic question of whether the United States remains the United States, or becomes gradually transformed into a province of the world-wide Soviet system."[6]

Another organization generally associated with the Radical Right is the Christian Crusade. This conservative, anti-Communist, religiously-oriented group is led by Rev. Billy James Hargis of Tulsa, Oklahoma. Though not as well known as the Birch Society, the Christian Crusade has been more aggressive in distributing literature, presenting radio and television programs, and organizing patriotic conferences. At one time the Crusade claimed that its activities included 600 fifteen-minute and 150 thirty-minute radio broadcasts per week, weekly television shows, fifteen to twenty large anti-Communist rallies per year, a weekly newspaper column known as "For and Against" which was sent to over 200 newspapers, plus the *Christian Crusade Magazine* with a reported circulation of 100,000. Indeed, Billy James Hargis was the power behind the first annual National Anti-Communist Leadership School, held in Tulsa, Oklahoma, in January, 1962. From the standpoint of energy expended, the Christian Crusade has in the past been a more formidable critic of the Court than has the Birch Society. It would appear, however, that the Crusade's influence and activities are waning, as criticism of the Radical Right mounts around the country.

RELIGIOUS OVERTONES

Unlike the Birch Society, the Christian Crusade has not placed complete emphasis on a single campaign such as the impeachment of Earl Warren. Indeed, the anti-Court material flowing from this organization is not great when compared to the mass of information distributed with respect to fighting Communism at all levels. But even this relatively small concentration is significant, and the religious overtones make it even more potent by inferring those opposing the Christian Crusade are anti-God. As Hargis expresses it — "Our battle is Christ versus anti-Christ...We are in a holy crusade to preserve our beloved way of life against a dictatorial way of life, often godless socialism and/or Communism."[7]

In the *Weekly Crusader,* a small anti-Communist periodical edited by Billy James Hargis, one of the more pertinent articles, entitled "Danger Confronting the United States," was written by M.T. Phelps, a former justice from the Arizona Supreme Court. Phelps, using innuendo, chastises those persons who feel that the Constitution and the Bible are "outmoded and outworn."[8]   He does not mention the Supreme Court justices, but the tone of the article conveys the subject of his criticism. The Christian Crusade also rents out tapes promoting its particular political philosophy. Included among these is a recent one by Congressman Dale Alford entitled "The Attack on Our Constitution." Governor Orval Faubus of Arkansas also has a tape entitled "My Defense of States' Rights."

In a series of television shows, Hargis has conveyed his own ideas on the Court controversy.[9] In a message called the "Supreme Court Against America," the politico-religious leader attacked the Court for ignoring the internal Communist conspiracy. He referred to the Court's personnel as naïve, arguing that they were the "greatest single factor aiding the Communists," and that Congress must act to curb the Court before it is too late. This suggestion is also forthcoming in Hargis' book entitled *Communist America— Must It Be?*[10] Again, the disturbing factor is the implied association between criticism of the Court and godliness. Hargis ended his television show on the Supreme Court with a prayer that read: "We pray that Christians may feel their responsibility and join us in this holy crusade to save our nation."[11]

OTHER RIGHT-WING CRITICS

Of less magnitude than the John Birch Society and the Christian Crusade, but still effective within a concentrated area, are several weekly radio broadcasts that promulgate an ultra-conservative philosophy. John T. Flynn's "America's Future," Frank Kilpatrick's "The American Way," and Dean Clarence Manion's "Manion Forum" are the best known of these programs. The Manion Forum, in particular, has served as a channel for anti-Court criticism on numerous occasions. Included among the guests of Dean Manion, formerly of Notre Dame Law School, have been such notable conservatives as Senator James Eastland, who spoke on the "Supreme Court — A Revolutionary Tribunal." After Eastland had finished his condemnation of the judiciary, Manion, whose stature is great among conservatives, remarked that "nothing strikes more dangerously at our liberties than tampering with the Constitution by a Communist brain-washed Supreme Court."[12] On another occasion, after a Georgia state representative spoke on "State Sovereignty — Last Bastion Against Communism," Manion closed the program with "The perils of a Red-tinted Supreme Court are ably outlined in this powerful speech."[13]

Manion followed the congressional anti-Court line of attack when he staunchly supported the Jenner bill in 1958. While testifying in favor of the bill, he interpreted fifteen Court decisions involving Communists not only as examples of judicial legislation (which he abhorred), but also as "resulting anarchy where Congress and the States are left powerless to detect and/or correct the evil of Communist subversion,"[14] Even before the Jenner bill was conceived, Manion was aggressively attacking the Court for its continuous anti-states' rights trend. On March 25, 1956, he broadcast a message upholding the rights of states to incorporate the doctrine of "interposition" in order to nullify certain judicial decisions.[15] A month later, he reinforced this theme by discussing the *Nelson* case which he considered an example of "judicial legislation...destroying states' rights."[16] He reasoned that only a strong, "self-conscious Congress and vigilant sacrificial self-reliance on the part of the States can now save the American Republic."[17]

NAME LENDS PRESTIGE

Since Manion has neither organization nor finances comparable to the Birch Society and the Christian Crusade, his greatest influence probably comes from the prestige that his name lends to conservative causes. He is a member of the Council of the John Birch Society, is on the Board of Advisors and Endorsers of the Christian Crusade, and has participated in the Freedom Forum series of the National Education Program, to name a few.

Testifying in favor of the Jenner bill in 1958, in addition to Manion, was a parade of relatively unknown witnesses representing the

ultra-conservative groups in America. Of these groups one in particular stands out because of its extraordinary attack on the Court. The
organization referred to is the SPX Research Associates. SPX stands
for "Soviet Principle 10," [18] an alleged plan to break America's resistance without resorting to war. The Research Association is made up
of former military intelligence officers who claim to have been in contact with Russian officers during World War II. This group, headed
by Thomas R. Hutton, a reserve Air Force colonel and former editor
of the *Binghamton Press* in New York, submitted a special study on
the Supreme Court before the subcommittee holding hearings on the
Jenner bill. The report was printed as a separate appendix to the main
report on the hearing. The subcommittee claimed that the SPX study
came in too late to be printed in the major report. The fact remains,
however, that the SPX material was originally submitted on February
28, 1958. Subsequent material was included in the main report and
hence the speculative reason for not including it is that the subcommittee desired a separate printing which could be distributed more
widely.

The title of the SPX study is "The Supreme Court as an Instrument of Global Conquest." [19] The essence of the report is that the
Supreme Court constitutes the most "powerful and potentially deter-
minative instrument of the Communist global conquest." The Court
via its recent "pro-Communist" decisions is accused of invoking a
"paralytic stroke" in behalf of the Reds. The study does not question
the good intentions of the justices, but argues that the problem must
be measured by whether the results of decisions are furthering the
Communist cause. In this, the "research group" feels that the record
of the Court speaks for itself. The pattern of decisions coincides
"with the established patterns of global conquest by paralysis." [20]
Court rulings since the School Segregation cases are described as
giving aid and comfort to the enemy.

IMAGINATIVELY DRAFTED
In and of itself, the SPX report could probably have been dismissed since it consisted of little more than the imaginative speculation of its drafters. But its very incredibility coupled with the aura of
respectability given to it by J.G. Sourwine, counsel for the subcommittee, who referred to the study as a "scholarly piece of work,"
tended to exaggerate its importance. Submitted when the fear of internal subversion was running high in conservative circles, the report
loomed as a piece of evidence that required rebuttal. Senators Hennings (D. Mo.) and Watkins (R. Utah) went so far as to call for
an investigation of SPX Associates in order to counter any damage the

report might cause. Actually, the controversy spent itself almost immediately. The report never generated the great impact anticipated by some, and is now generally viewed as just another one of the more bitter and reckless attacks.

FAVORED JENNER BILL

Numerous other small organizations of the Radical Right testified in favor of Senator Jenner's attempt to limit the appellate jurisdiction of the Court. The National Economic Council (1600 members), headed by Merwin K. Hart, was among the more prominent of these groups. The N.E.C., supporting "private enterprise and American independence," focused its attacks on the premise that the Court was leading the country toward a state of world federalism. This testimony, offered by Merwin Hart in support of the Court-curbing legislation, was in line with the philosophy expounded by the N.E.C. in its bi-monthly *Economic Council Letter*.[21] During the 1957-58 Court controversy, the *Economic Council Letter* noted that the Supreme Court had "practically wrecked" the means which Congress and the people had built up to fight Communism. This was supposedly accomplished by a "whole string of judicial decisions...including the *Jencks* case which nearly destroyed the usefulness of the F.B.I."[22] With respect to the *Watkins* decisions, the *Letter* concluded that if the "majority opinion had been written in the Kremlin, it could hardly have better served the cause of Communism."[23] Three years later, the NEC again voiced its displeasure with the Court in its *Letter* entitled "Where We Stand Today."[24] In surveying the progress of the nation, the NEC chastised the Court for its holding in the School Segregation cases, and its tendency to "advance the objectives of the Kremlin."[25] Next to the Executive department, the Court supposedly constituted the "best ally of Communism in the United States."

OTHER GROUPS INVOLVED

The American Coalition of Patriotic Societies (claiming three million members), the Defenders of the American Constitution, the Ladies of the Grand Army of the Republic, and the Women's Patriotic Conference on National Defense (representing nineteen organizations) were among other organizations urging passage of the Jenner bill in order to curb the "usurpation" of the Court.

In similar vein, the representative of the Conservative Party of New Jersey referred to the justices as "nine legal delinquents."[26] Andrew Wilson Green, an attorney, reinforced this line of attack by noting that there are those who suspect one member of the Court as being under the Communist discipline, another as being subject to

Communist blackmail, another as knowingly following Communist desire out of political ambition, another as being sympathetic because so many of his friends are Communist, including members of his family, and a fifth as being motivated by resentment of a religious nature.[27] Green protected himself under examination by referring to these as suspicions currently in the mind of the public. The subcommittee dignified the reckless and baseless testimony by permitting it to go on for twenty-four pages.

Edgar C. Bundy, of the Abraham Lincoln National Republican Club, said his organization was desperately concerned over the fact that the judiciary was giving aid and comfort to the enemy.[28] George J. Thomas, representing the Congress of Freedom (comprised of the delegates of some 500 separate organizations), interpreted the recent Supreme Court decisions as "national red lights of warning of the destruction of our government and our liberties...."[29] In addition, Thomas went on to attack the law clerk system which "has a leftist tendency" as well as Justice Frankfurter and the late Justice Holmes for "utter contempt for God, and the ideal of God."

Another relatively unknown spokesman of the radical right is the *Independent American*. This newspaper styles itself as a conservative "pro-American" action newspaper which reprints the "best " in conservative thought and opinion every month. It advocates formation of a new conservative political party, and is unflaggingly anti-Communist. The *Independent American* is run by Kent and Phoebe Courtney of New Orleans who align themselves closely with Robert Welch and the Birch Society. This newspaper is so far to the right that it has chastised even the conservative *National Review* for "not keeping up on its homework." William Buckley, editor of the *National Review*, is described as the "sophomore savant of the right."[30]

IMPEACHMENT CAMPAIGN

Like the John Birch Society, the *Independent American* has concentrated on a campaign to impeach Chief Justice Warren. One of the techniques used by the organization in its campaign was the distribution of a pamphlet entitled "On Whose Side is the U.S. Supreme Court?"[31] Included in the pamphlet is a copy of Senator Eastland's box scores showing the voting records of the various justices in cases involving Communists. Eastland's scores are supplemented by headings in bright red stating "Congressional Investigations Crippled," "Professors Free to Teach Communism," "States Prevented From Controlling Reds," and "Supreme Court Refuses to Recognize Red Menace."

Another pamphlet distributed was entitled "Impeach Earl Warren," supposedly a documented record of Warren's pro-Communist rulings.[32] This is highlighted by large red subtitles announcing "Warren for Communists as Attorneys," "Warren Votes to Allow Communists Free to Carry Out Subversion," and others. The pamphlet concludes with an outline of measures that can be taken to assist in the program to impeach Earl Warren.

The Courtneys also provide a news commentary over thirty-three radio stations in fifteen states (only three of which are not in the South). Even with this combined media approach, however, it is doubtful whether the *Independent American* movement on its own reaches a significant number of people.[33]

DAN SMOOT REPORTS

One of Kent and Phoebe Courtney's conservative colleagues is Dan Smoot, an ex-FBI agent who works out of Dallas, Texas. His weekly periodical, the *Dan Smoot Report*, is not unlike the *Independent American* from a political standpoint. In addition to the weekly publication, the Smoot report is transmitted on forty television stations in twelve states, and seventy radio stations in twenty states. Its philosophy advocates abandoning social security and welfare-state programs, boycotting Russia, invading Cuba, and impeaching Earl Warren. On January 30, 1961, at the same time the Birch Society was instituting its campaign, the *Dan Smoot Report* began a series of two studies on the "Impeachment of Earl Warren."[34] This report was supposed to present ample evidence to sustain the anti-Warren allegations. Smoot attacked Warren for not having a sufficient background to be a justice-of-the-peace, let alone a Chief Justice of the Supreme Court. In addition, he claimed that Warren was "abysmally ignorant" in the field of Constitutional Law, a socialist, and in favor of unlimited governmental expansion. Smoot examined a number of Supreme Court decisions, beginning with the School Segregation cases, and concluded that Warren's voting record in and of itself was sufficient evidence for purposes of impeachment. Smoot claimed that he could call upon thirty-six state Supreme Court chief justices, members of the A.B.A. Committee on Communist Tactics, Strategy, and Objectives, as well as a host of congressmen as witnesses in the impeachment proceedings.

The attacks on the Court by the *Independent American* and the *Dan Smoot Report* are extreme indeed, but the fact remains that such emotional non-analytical appeals are beginning to receive a great deal of financial backing.[35] In combination, the forces of the Radical Right today may well be reaching a significant number of people, especially in the South and Southwest.

OVER-INTENSE ATTACKS

A uniquely vivid example of the vitriolic tone of the Radical Right may be found in the book previously mentioned, *Nine Men Against America,* by Rosalie Gordon.[36] The author traces the "historical disintegration" of the Supreme Court from the time of President Franklin Roosevelt. With respect to the old guard — Justices Butler, Sutherland, McReynolds, and Van Devanter, she felt that whatever their philosophy, it was "basically American." In examining the various justices, Black is condemned for being more favorable to Communists than to American businessmen, Frankfurter as an "opportunistic thinker," and Douglas as no more than a publicity seeker and an "out and out leftist." These justices, she argued, "went about their demolition job on the Constitution in the manner characteristic of our social revolutionaries for the past twenty years."[37] Former Justices Jackson, Burton, and Reed were referred to as the "not-so-liberal group."

Miss Gordon examines the School Segregation cases and the other controversial public offender cases and condemns the Court for its holdings, also attacking the law clerk system because the clerks come from schools which have been "infiltrated," and in some cases "saturated with left-wing thinking." One half of the eighteen clerks were recruited from "hotbeds of New Deal-collectivist-left-wing" schools such as Harvard and Yale.[38]

Miss Gordon's attack upon the Court is so intense that it may fail to make its point with the average reader. Indeed, although it certainly reinforced the anti-Court thinking of the Radical Right, it is doubtful that the book received much if any circulation outside of that group.

THE TRADITIONAL CRITICS

Whereas the Radical Right claimed Rosalie Gordon as an authoritative commentator, the traditional conservatives looked to men such as George Sokolsky, Raymond Moley, Fulton Lewis Jr., and David Lawrence. Even Arthur Krock of the *New York Times* qualifies as one of the Court's traditional major critics, though this claim is somewhat tempered by the subtlety of his comment. Of these Lawrence has acted outstandingly as the conservative champion in the recent attacks.

His stand is somewhat paradoxical. Only twenty-five years ago he authored a book entitled *Supreme Court or Political Puppets*[39] in which he defended the conservative Court of the thirties against the threat of F.D.R.'s Court-packing advocates. He rationalizes this conspicuous reversal by stating that for twenty years the Court has been packed with justices "selected from a cult that believes the Constitution can be rewritten at will by the judiciary."[40] In view of the fact that the settled law of the past supposedly is being pushed aside, Lawrence reasons that the Court must be checked by limiting the tenure of the offices, requiring judicial experience, and requiring amendments to change the Constitution. "By their decisions," he has stated, "they twist the Constitution out of its accustomed and natural meaning... When they do this, they provoke widespread condemnation."[41]

Though Lawrence wields influence among his conservative colleagues, his chief value to the Court-curbing cause is derived from his *apparent* editorial control of *U.S. News and World Report,* a magazine with a circulation of about 1,350,000. In spite of the fact that the publication expressly disclaims this control,[42] there are many who feel that he does influence the tone of the publication. In any case, there is a strong, consistent conservatism which permeates the weekly.

Numerous articles and editorials have dealt with the Court-curbing issue, the majority of them reflecting an anti-Court attitude. Lawrence himself has provided the foundation upon which to build a campaign with editorials entitled "Twenty Years of Court Packing,"[43] "Treason's Greatest Victory,"[44] and "Eroding the Forty-Eight States."[45] In addition, the magazine has offered articles by such anti-Court advocates as Senator John Stennis (D. Miss.),[46] and former Supreme Court Justice James Byrnes,[47] among others. This anti-Court tone has been reinforced on occasions with supposedly unbiased articles such as "How Judges Feel About the Supreme Court,"[48] and "Who Writes Decisions of the Supreme Court?"[49]

ANTI-COURT LEADERSHIP

The *National Review* has provided even greater leadership for the anti-Court segment of the press. This traditionally conservative bi-weekly with a circulation of about 85,000 boasts the talents of such spokesmen as William Buckley, James Burnham, and especially L. Brent Bozell. Bozell represented the *National Review* in testifying in favor of the Jenner bill in 1958. The associate editor suggested that no one wanted to curb the Court simply because of a disagreement but rather because the Court did not stay within its jurisdiction.[50] Bozell felt that the Court had immobilized the U.S. program of national security, thereby incurring the "popular disrespect of our people." After discussing the *National Review's* differences with certain decisions, Bozell attacked the justices for deciding cases in advance on political grounds, and then looking for ways to justify their holdings.

Forrest Davis contributed an article entitled "The Court Reaches

for Total Power,"[51] in which he examined the controversial decisions of
the Court and concluded that the Communists were the only bene-
ficiaries of these decisions. Davis did not stop at this point. He proceeded to attack several of the justices for "leftist" leanings and
suspected "lack of integrity." A similar attack on the Court made by
Marian Stephenson used the box-score device to show how the justices had voted in cases involving suspected Communists.[52] For the
most part, however, the articles in the *National Review* did not show a
propensity to be overly emotional.

In one article Associate Editor Bozell took issue with the John
Birch Society, contending that there simply were no grounds upon
which to base an impeachment of Earl Warren.[53] The remedy, according to Bozell, lay with Congress in limiting the appellate jurisdiction
of the Court, or possibly in censure. The *National Review* never sacrificed the opportunity to turn a literary phrase. Bozell referred to Warren as a ".partisan agent of fashionable ideology," and accused the
Chief Justice of "juridical sloth and political tendentiousness" which
left the law in a state of confusion. Other articles showing the general
trend of thinking in the *National Review* include: "Why Not Investigate the Court?"[54] "Can Congressional Investigations Survive Watkins?"[55] "A Bill to Curb the Court,"[56] and "Court or Constitution:
The Supreme Court's Steady Usurpation."[57]

There are several other conservative periodicals which have been
active in the anti-Court campaign. *Human Events*, with a circulation
reported to be around 90,000,[58] follows much the same line as that of
*National *Review*, but lacks both the prestige and influence which
that periodical enjoys as a spokesman for the conservative cause.
This weekly pamphlet has focused most of its attention on the issue
that the Court was becoming a third legislature. Included among its
contributors is Rosalie Gordon, who writes for the John Birch Society.
Typical of the articles found in *Human Events* are: "When the Court
is Not Supreme," "The Web of Warren," "Behind the Black Robes,"
"America's Constitutional Crisis," and "The Supreme Court Marches
On — To the Left."

Farm and Ranch Magazine, owned and published by Thomas J.
Anderson with a circulation reported to be nearly 1.3 million, is another member of the conservative press which has consistently attacked
the Court. In an article entitled "Straight Talk" by Anderson, it is argued that the members of the Court have "forfeited their right to life
tenure and should be made directly responsible to Congress and the
People."[59] Anderson argued that the "political justices are now account-
able to no one but themselves." *Farm and Ranch Magazine* has been

one of the more prominent contributors to the anti-Communist crusade of the Radical Right. Its effectiveness from an editorial standpoint is lessened, however, since it is not a "news" magazine.

NEWSPAPERS PARTICIPATE

In addition to weekly and monthly periodicals, the daily newspapers have played a significant role in criticizing the Supreme Court. It is not uncommon to find the newspapers framing their editorial attacks against the Court in especially colorful language, for the reader-interest and sales value.

The response of a number of conservative newspapers to the public offender decisions involving Communism gives an insight into some of the critical editorials. The *New York Herald Tribune* (circulation 488,000), after analyzing the *Jencks* case stated the "The whole American corporate structure is shaken." [60] The *Chicago New World* (circulation not published) commented:

> If the day comes when we all join hands and rattle our chains in a slave mart, or rather our bones in a Red grave dug with our own hands, we may find ourselves repeating in unpleasant tones the names of some of the present members of the Court. [61]

Equally bitter was an editorial in Columbia, South Carolina, which stated that "In the exercise of dictatorial powers, the difference between the Kremlin and the Supreme Court is that the Kremlin is composed of eleven men and the Supreme Court only nine." [62] With reference to the *Jencks* decision, the *Fort Lauderdale Sunday News* (circulation 62,000) characterized the judiciary as "our Alice-in-Wonderland Supreme Court," while the *New York Daily News* (circulation 3,200,000) simply referred to *Jencks* as a "Supreme Court Blunder." [63]

The reaction of the conservative press to the School Prayer case was mixed, with most papers regretful that such a decision had to be made. There were a few notable dissents, however. The *Los Angeles Times* (circulation 1,165,396) felt that the justices had been persuaded by a "small group of guardhouse sophists to make a burlesque show of the world's first complete declaration of religious toleration." In San Francisco, the *News-Call Bulletin* (circulation 175,000) felt the Supreme Court acted in "the most narrow legalistic sense" while in New York, the *Journal American* (circulation 812,000) urged immediate passage of a Constitutional amendment to rectify this "deprivation of liberty." The *Raleigh News and Observer* (circulation 149,132) felt the decision interpreted the Constitution "with a rigidity which is ridiculous." [64] The majority of newspapers, however, appeared to be exceptionally calm over an issue which in many quarters seemed emotionally provocative.

CLAIM INTEREST GROUPS

The traditional conservative critics also claimed the allegiance of a number of well-organized interest groups. The American Legion, with a membership of nearly three million, is a conservative octogenarian. Although at the 1957 annual national convention the Legion went on record against many of the Court decisions, no representative testified in favor of the Jenner bill, because the 1957 resolutions were not so phrased that the Legion could back S. 2646. The resolutions in point simply announced that the Legion deplored the specific Supreme Court decisions which endangered national security and assisted law violators. They further urged Congress to establish by law the basic qualifications to be met by federal judgeship appointees.[65]

Just prior to the convention, the *American Legion Magazine* carried an article entitled "Relief for American Reds."[66] This examined the decisions of "Red Monday" and the response of the Communist press. It concluded that "If these decisions stand without legislative correction — they will represent the greatest blow ever struck against civil liberties in this country in time of peace."[67]

Other articles in American Legion publications have generated anti-Court feeling. Eugene Lyons wrote a review entitled "Why the Reds are Gaining in America"[68] for the *American Legion Magazine*, while similar blasts have appeared in the *Firing Line*, a bi-monthly publication distributed by the National American Commission of the American Legion.[69] Although the general tone of these articles is not inflammable, they do constitute a continuous campaign against Communism. The Legion is afraid of Communist penetration in religion, the schools, the theatre — in every social institution or situation.

Hence the Supreme Court decisions which the Legionnaires feel condone Communist activity are bound to incur the organization's wrath.

DAR TAKES A STAND

The Daughters of the American Revolution in 1957 submitted a resolution to Congress in which it criticized the Court for its stand on numerous public offender cases as well as on the right-to-work issue. It urged Congress to take action to limit the power of the Court. One year later, the D.A.R. again called for a resolution to curb the Court, and urged that the justices be required to have at least five years' judicial experience before qualifying for the Supreme Court.[70] The Veterans of Foreign Wars went a step further than the D.A.R. in actively supporting the Jenner bill. At their 1957 national convention, the V.F.W. adopted a resolution to the effect that recent Supreme Court decisions protected the Communist conspiracy to the extent that immediate legislation was badly needed.[71] Francis J. McNamara, Assistant Director of the National Legislative Service of the V.F.W., cautioned the subcommittee that after the enactment of the Jenner bill, the appellate courts, in the event they acted as the Supreme Court had, would have to be dealt with in like manner.[72] Apparently the V.F.W. would eliminate judicial review entirely in order to combat the threat of internal subversion.

Whereas the veterans' groups published resolutions, the National Association of Manufacturers and the Chamber of Commerce exert subtle private pressures on Congressmen. While their interest generally is tied to economics, several of the decisions involving preemption and states' rights did provide these large pressure groups with an opportunity to promote their respective causes. Walter Murphy has traced the influence exerted by the Chamber of Commerce, the N.A.M., and the American Farm Bureau Federation on Congress in reference to H.R. 3 (anti-pre-emption bill) in his book *Congress and the Court.*[73] Indeed these large interest groups readily make themselves felt in silent behind-the-scenes maneuvers.

Among interest-group responses, mention must be made of religious organizations. Analysis in this area is difficult because of the divisive stands within particular groups. Of the Catholic publications, *Commonweal* has acted as a liberal spokesman, generally praising the Court's decisions, while *America* has taken a much more conservative view. The intra-sect split is also revealed in the *Voice of St. Jude's* which criticized other Catholic publications for taking the Court to task over public offender decisions.[74]

There was more uniformity among Catholics, however, with respect to the School Prayer decision. Roman Catholic clergy were adamant in their criticism of the Court's position. Cardinal Spellman stated that he was "shocked." Cardinal McIntyre viewed the holding as "scandalizing" and one which "puts shame on our faces as we are forced to emulate Mr. Khrushchev."[75] *America* characterized the decision as "stupid . . . a doctrinaire decision, an unrealistic decision, a decision that spits in the face of our history, our tradition, and our heritage as a religious people."[76]

The Protestant clergy were somewhat varied, yet predominately negative in their responses. Dr. Byrant Kirkland of the Presbyterian Church was concerned over the Supreme Court's favoring a "completely secular state," and felt that the decision might weaken the moral basis of our democracy. Evangelist Billy Graham viewed the Court's decision as another step toward secularization and felt that the framers of the Constitution desired freedom *of* religion, not freedom *from* religion.[77] Bishop James Pike of the California Protestant Episcopal diocese expressed "surprise" that the Court had extended the First Amendment to a non-sectarian prayer. He felt that the Court had misread and distorted the meaning of the First Amendment.[78] The Jewish and Unitarian faiths generally approved of the decision.

5. THE STATE CRITICS

Attacks on the Supreme Court from state agencies are less evident, but just as real as attacks from other sources. For the most part these attacks have been channeled through Congressional representatives in keeping with the state agencies' practice of gaining greater public recognition by using Congress as their arena. In view of this, the number of judicial attacks upon the Court emanating from these agencies is somewhat limited, and the general nature of criticism is not easy to ascertain. Certainly the conservative state legislatures are in disagreement with the prevailing social philosophy of the Court. But "discordant social philosophy" does not constitute the only base for the states' discontent. Equally important is the problem of "intra-governmental conflict." Over the years gradually, the federal government has become the focal point of political power in the United States. At the same time, there are many who feel that the states have been relegated to a diminished power position vis-à-vis the federal government. This supposed loss of relative power by the states has sensitized them to holdings of the Court which have tended to crystallize or point up the loss.

For the most part, the state agencies are result-oriented critics. Their goal appears to be rectification of some of the more controversial decisions which have been distasteful to them. Several of the Southern states have attempted to bring about rectification by legal myth — the doctrine of interposition — designed to circumvent the Court's decisions in particular areas. Commanding little if any legal recognition, interposition did serve as a basis upon which to rationalize the South's non-compliance with the decrees of the Court.

The School Segregation cases gave the impetus to state attacks upon the Court. Though the groundwork for the decisions had been laid earlier in *Sweatt v. Painter* [1] and *McLaurin v. Oklahoma State Regents*,[2] the reaction in Southern states was almost one of shock. The Florida legislature quickly submitted a resolution to Congress denouncing the "usurpation of power" by the Supreme Court.[3]

It demanded that action be taken by Congress to eliminate the life-tenure of Supreme Court justices. Finally, Florida urged a change in the Tenth Amendment of the Constitution to define specifically the powers reserved to the states.

Tennessee submitted a like resolution to the Judiciary Committee condemning the "oppressive usurpation" of the Court,[4] which was characterized as having shown "grievous and deplorable" disrespect for the Constitution. Tennessee manifested concern also over Court personnel. South Carolina went so far as to campaign for Congress to enact legislation to secure a body of judicially experienced and "in every respect qualified persons" for positions on the Court.[5] They suggested that the conservative American Bar Association submit a list of fifty qualified candidates for the President's consideration whenever a vacancy on the Bench occurred.

SCHOOL DECISIONS ARE TARGETS

Among the key targets of the Southern states during this period were the criteria used by the Supreme Court in deciding *Brown v. Board of Education*. The Florida legislature assailed the decision on the grounds that the sociological, economic, and political ideas of the justices did not constitute a sufficient basis for decision.[6] Illustrating this type of attack, which was often bitter and in many instances irrelevant, was a speech by Governor Griffin of Georgia to a Citizen's Council at Greenville, Mississippi. He condemned the federal government for bringing Gunnar Myrdal, "a known socialist who had served the Communist cause," to the United States in 1937 in order to examine the Negro problem. Out of Myrdal's study, of course, came his book, *An American Dilemma*, one of the sources which the Court alluded to in the School Segregation decision. Citing a statement by Senator Eastland to the effect that "The Court took the writings and teachings of pro-Communist agitators and people who are part and parcel of the Red conspiracy and substituted them for the law of the land," [7] Griffin went on to attack Myrdal for squandering U.S. funds throughout the underdeveloped world, an issue not relevant to the School Segregation cases. Thus it was attempted to stigmatize the *Brown* decision by discredit-through-association.

When sticking to the subject, many of the state critics tended to lose themselves in glittering generalities. Witness the statements of former Governor Herman Talmadge of Georgia who noted that the Court had relegated the Constitution to a "mere scrap of paper." With reference to the *Brown* decision, Talmadge charged that the Court had "ignored all law and precedent and usurped from Congress and the people the power to amend the Constitution." There remained, he said, only the question as to "whether to cut off our heads with a sharp knife or a dull one."[8] The next year, when the issue of segregation was merged with that of Communism, the Georgia legislature passed a resolution calling for the impeachment of Warren, Black, Douglas, Reed, Frankfurter, and Clark,[9] on the claim that these justices had given aid and comfort to the enemy, and were guilty of high crimes and misdemeanors "too numerous to mention."

CHALLENGE FROM THE HARD CORE

Perhaps the boldest response to the controversial decisions of the Court came in the form of a direct challenge to the decrees of the judiciary by several of the hard-core Southern states. On February 9, 1956, the Georgia legislature adopted a resolution "interposing" the sovereignty of Georgia in any situation in which Georgia felt the Court was exercising a power not granted it by the Constitution.[10] The doctrine of interposition was based on the concept that the powers of the federal government, including the Supreme Court, resulted from a compact with the several states. Any power not a result of this Constitutional compact had no effect upon the sovereign states. Virginia passed a similar resolution on the same day,[11] and so did Mississippi,[12] Alabama,[13] South Carolina,[14] and Louisiana.[15] The application of the doctrine was a temporary rallying point for Southern critics. Though many observers felt that the doctrine had terminated with the Civil War, it did serve to usher in an era of non-compliance with Court decrees, and is an example of the lengths to which some states were willing to go in terms of disagreement with the Court's social philosophy.

In marked contrast is the *modus operandi* of several state commissions concerned with the promotion of states' rights. The most influential and effective of these is the Virginia Commission on Constitutional Government which publishes a series of "historical statements and papers expounding the role of the States in their relation to the central government." Beautifully bound and written in scholarly fashion, these reports present anti-Court arguments in the subtlest of fashions. Historical statements such as "The Fort Hill Address of John C. Calhoun," "Thomas Jefferson on Constitutional Issues," and "The Kentucky-Virginia Resolutions and Mr. Madison's Report of 1799," support the traditionally conservative approach to Constitutional issues, which, had it been followed by the Court, might have reaffirmed the holding in *Plessy v. Ferguson*. These scholarly statements are amplified with other researches such as "Did the Court Interpret or Amend?", "Equality vs. Liberty: The Eternal Conflict," "A Question of Intent — The States, Their Schools and the Fourteenth Amendment" all expressing sophisticated and thoughtful opposition to the moderately liberal trend of decisions.

GOVERNORS ARE CONCERNED

State governors are a group concerned with the problem of federal-state relations and have expressed their displeasure with the growing federal power. The breadth of the governors' concern extends to labor relations, state taxation, interstate commerce, welfare legislation, and subversive activities, to name but a few.

Pre-emption has always been a provocative word to the state governors. The case of *Pennsylvania v. Nelson*[16] seemed climactic on this topic. It dealt with a decision by the Court to preclude the states from enforcing their sedition laws in the area of federal competence. The state governors, at their forty-eighth annual conference, not only declared opposition to the Court's opinion but also called upon Congress to draft its laws so that they could not be construed as preempting state laws.[17]

In 1962, another sensitive Constitutional issue was presented to the governors with the rendering of the School Prayer case. At first, the conference was indecisive. A resolution was offered by Governors Bryant of Florida and Reed of Maine urging Congress to adopt a Constitutional amendment "to make clear beyond challenge, the acknowledgement of our nation and people in their faith in God." The resolution just barely passed the required percentage needed to send it to committee. Finally, however, the conference unanimously endorsed the proposed Constitutional amendment by vote.[18]

Resolutions emanating from governors' conferences are inevitably phrased in exceedingly general terms. This of course dilutes their effectiveness. But it must be remembered that governors are reluctant to get out on a political limb if the diverse interests at such a conference can be reconciled on a generality basis.[19]

The largest controversy over criticism of judicial decisions from a state standpoint was sparked by the 1958 Conference of state chief justices. The conference, by a vote of 36-8, adopted a report of the Committee on Federal-State Relationships as Affected by Judicial Decisions, and this endorsement became the subject of much debate. The report seemed to be predicated on an erroneous interpretation of five monographs written by members of the University of Chicago Law

School on federal-state relations.[20] After laying an adequate diplomatic foundation to the effect that "respect for the law does not preclude disagreement" with Supreme Court pronouncements, the report criticized the Court for lack of judicial self-restraint.[21] This was stressed in relation to the Court's tendency to become a "policymaker." It is here that the conference felt "the greatest restraint is called for."[22]

POWER EXPANSION FEARED

The major theme was the state Chief Justices' displeasure with those rulings supposedly fostering the expansion of national power. The report hazily alluded to the Court's invalidation of conservative economic policies, including problems dealing with labor relations, grants-in-aid, and commerce in general. It expressed concern about the Court's holding in a number of public offender cases in which states were involved. Included among these were the controversial *Nelson, Sweezy, Konigsberg, and Schware* decisions, in addition to a number of state criminal cases.

Immediate reaction was mixed. Several members of the Bar and legal academicians were disturbed because this criticism of the Court came at a time when the High Bench needed every supporter it could get. The country was literally being inundated with negative commentary on the Court from vocal conservative congressmen and interest groups. The state Chief Justices created a fresh wind to fan the flames of criticism, and raised the temperature of the blaze which had appeared to be cooling down. In a sense they placed a mantle of legitimacy and respectability upon what was largely emotional and irrational criticism.

REPORT ASTOUNDING

In addition to the public, who were impressed, many attorneys and academicians were astounded at the manner and tone of the report. To say that the Supreme Court too often had tended to adopt the "role of policy-maker without proper judicial restraint" was to mislead the public. The Court's role as a "policy-maker" is undoubtedly accepted by most of the Chief Justices, but this phrase has been used to attack the Court by critics who have little if any knowledge of the judiciary's proper function. Surely the Chief Justices were well aware of this while drafting their report, and there are other passages which suggest that the Chief Justices really did intend to chastise the Court. For example, the following — concerning the Court's personnel:

These frequent differences and occasional overrulings of prior decisions in Constitutional cases cause us grave concern as to whether individual views of the members of the court...do not unconsciously override a more dispassionate consideration of what is or is not constitutionally warranted.[23]

Subtle as it may be, this statement constitutes an indictment of some of the justices, and reinforces the attacks of those conservative critics who have used the judicial personality as a main target. Substantiating this premise is another statement to the effect that when the Court becomes a policy-maker, "it may leave construction behind and exercise functions which are essentially legislative in character ..."[24] The state justices attribute this to the fact that the Court at times "is impatient with the slow workings of our federal system" and is unwilling to wait for Congress to exercise its intended function. Finally, the Court is taken to task for its occasional abandonment of the doctrine of *stare decisis.* "It seems strange," the report states, "that under a Constitutional doctrine which requires all others to recognize the Supreme Court's rulings on Constitutional questions as binding...the Court itself has so frequently overturned its own decisions..."[25]

CRITICISM OFTEN SHALLOW

In many instances, the criticism of the state judges was predicated on shallow grounds. In the first place, as many authorities have pointed out,[26] the Supreme Court for the most part has used great restraint in the areas explored by the report. Even in *Pennsylvania v. Nelson,* which so concerned the conference, the Supreme Court deferred to the highest court in Pennsylvania by affirming the State Supreme Court decision. It has also deferred generally to the states with respect to state taxation of interstate commerce, intergovernmental immunities permitting a greater freedom for state taxation, and state regulation of interstate commerce in the absence of federal legislation.[27] Professor John Schmidhauser further points out that it has really been the state courts which have been "judicially active" in striking down encroaching welfare legislation passed by state legislatures.[28] This poses the question as to whether the state chief justices were concerned for the exercise of judicial self-restraint as a cherished legal attribute, or for the clash of their social and political ideas with those expressed by the Supreme Court.

DEFERENCE NOT NOTED

Neither did the 1958 conference note that the Supreme Court has been exceptionally deferential to the national legislature. For the past twenty-five years, the Court has exercised considerable judicial self-restraint in allowing Congress to experiment, thereby expanding national power. Dean Lockhart of Minnesota Law School suggested that the conference of state Chief Justices ended up criticizing the wrong agency. The real villain in the concentration of national power has not been the Supreme Court; rather, it has been Congress.

The question remains open as to what actually provoked the Chief Justices. A principal motivation lay in the radically divergent social philosophies pointed up by recent liberal decisions. There is some evidence in the report itself that many of the Chief Justices would have turned the clock back to the pre-1937 era when the national judiciary assumed a more *laissez faire* attitude toward economic problems. The state judges have reflected a distinctly conservative philosophy as a whole, as is borne out by the 1958 report. Professor Harold Chase notes also, from Chief Justice Jones' minority report, that much of the conference's criticism could be attributed to lingering dissatisfaction with the School Segregation cases.[29] Undoubtedly the Southern bloc constituted a formidable pressure group within the state judges' conference.

"Intra-governmental conflict" also is apparent in the criticism of the Chief Justices. A main theme of the report was concern over the expansion of federal authority and the alleged consequent contraction of state power, and with the threat of a role diminished in importance for the State Supreme Courts or their equivalent. Further, because the U.S. Supreme Court has enjoyed a greater prestige generally than the highest courts of the several states, there may be a trace of jealousy among the state justices. This, combined with a firm distaste for the so-called liberal fibre of Supreme Court opinions, makes the conference attack on the Court more comprehensible.

Although it is always proper and even desirable, to have the decisions of the Court challenged and tested to see that they are in tune with the times, the criticism of the Court by the conference of state Chief Justices was not "judiciously presented" and failed, therefore to fulfill its function.

Furthermore, it gave support and an aura of respectability to a number of reckless attacks directed toward the Court in the same year.[30]

6. LAW ENFORCEMENT CRITICS

The law enforcement agencies have been among the more influential groups engaged in criticizing the Warren Court. While disturbed with the social philosophy emanating from the High Bench, these agencies are primarily concerned with the problem of "decisional obstruction" — that is the restrictions which the certain Supreme Court decisions have placed upon law enforcement — decisions which supposedly have hindered these agencies in the performance of their duties.

Decisions in the *Mallory* and *Jencks* cases (analyzed in Chapter 3) were regarded as interfering with full and free exercise of the respective functions of the various law enforcement agencies. The *Mallory* decision, which invalidated a confession if it was obtained during an unreasonable delay between the time a criminal was apprehended and the time of his arraignment, set off a barrage of protests to the effect that the police no longer could fight crime adequately. The *Jencks* decision, which permitted the inspection of confidential statements held by the FBI for purposes of impeaching a witness, generated a like response from the Federal Bureau of Investigation. The FBI felt this decision would make it impossible to secure evidence from confidential informers who feared exposure.

The *Mallory* decision provoked a special congressional investigation of methods that might be adopted to rectify the Court's seemingly narrow interpretation.[1] Most of the testimony presented before the investigating committee, headed by Senator Hennings (D. Mo.), was unemotional and scholarly in tone, genuinely aimed at preserving the spirit behind the *Mallory* decision, and at the same time making certain that police investigations would not be unduly hampered.

EXCEPTIONS CONSPICUOUS

There were some conspicuous exceptions to the dispassionate approach. Robert V. Murray, Washington chief of police, in what appeared to be an exaggerated distortion of police capabilities, stated that most of the "murders, the rapes, and robberies that I have come in contact with would have gone unsolved and unpunished under the *Mallory* decision."[2] He estimated further that 90 percent of the professional criminals would have escaped punishment under the restrictions imposed by *Mallory*.

Edgar E. Scott, Murray's deputy chief, went even further than his boss. Scott accused the Court of forgetting the rights of the law-abiding public, "the family of the deceased, and the victim of the rapist."[3] He felt the effect of the decision would be to "encourage the professional criminal to commit the crime again." In expanding his criticism to include the members of the Court, Scott said that he thought it would be well "to examine some of these persons to see what selfish interest they might have in seeking to make it easy to get criminals off." He concluded by stating that now we find "some who are trying to punish the police. . . ."[4]

CRITICISM IS SEVERE

Such bitter criticism was not a common occurrence before the Hennings Committee, but was rather prevalent among law enforcement officers elsewhere. At the convention of the International Association of Police in Honolulu, 1957, the Supreme Court was severely criticized for the *Mallory* decision. Chief Francis J. Ahern of San Francisco referred to a growing attitude resulting in the repression of workable crime prevention programs.[5] This was echoed by Chief Alfred Smalley of Highland Park, New Jersey, who asserted that the recent Supreme Court decisions were a threat to law and order. He further commented that there was an "influential minority in this country intent on destroying law enforcement by raising the question of (individual) rights."[6] Keynote speaker, the late Chief William H. Parker of Los Angeles, noted that the "new birth of freedom" since World War II had stirred forces which "either as a fetish or as a concealed assault upon authority, espoused the cause of what has now been dubbed theoretical individual rights."[7]

Such reprimands notwithstanding, the main concern of the law enforcement agencies was to eliminate the rule promulgated in the

Mallory decision in order that the police could apprehend criminals more freely. The Sheriff's Association of Texas adopted a resolution urging Congress to take the necessary steps in restoring to law enforcement officers the necessary tools for criminal investigation.[8] Joseph D. Lohman, sheriff of Cook County, Illinois, asked Congress to spell out precisely what police officials were able to do.[9] He even wanted the legislature to define psychological and physical duress, believing that only in this way could law enforcement officers actually know the lengths to which they might go in crime prevention.

Professor Fred Inbau of Northwestern University testified before the Hennings Committee that he thought the Court was somewhat "out-of-line" in its holding in *Mallory*, and also that the Courts should not assume the burden of setting up standards for improvement of police procedures. Professor Inbau, who has always been a strong supporter of law enforcement agencies, argued that the "courts ought to put the handcuffs away."[10] District Attorney Francis Coakley of Alameda County, California, testified along similar lines and urged that the courts stop making the police "whipping boys."[11]

All in all, the critics believed that the Court had simply extended too narrow an interpretation to the concept of "unreasonable delay." In fact, the Court had done no more than apply its interpretation of the *McNabb* rule to fit the facts of the *Mallory* situation. Thus it appears that *Mallory* did no more than rekindle an old controversy which had plagued law enforcement officers for a number of years.

DISPUTE WITH FBI

Since the *Jencks* decision called for the disclosure of confidential files of the FBI under certain circumstances, the Federal Bureau of Investigation was one of the primary organizations campaigning to change that law. J. Edgar Hoover, naturally, wanted to defend the position of "confidential informants." According to his figures these undisclosed sources of information had enabled the FBI to arrest more than 2,700 persons in 1956.[12] Hoover claimed that "The very basis of our success is the FBI's assurance to this country's citizens that the information they give will be maintained in the strictest confidence in our files."[13] Former Attorney General Herbert Brownell supported Hoover's contention, stating that law enforcement would be almost impossible unless Congress limited the scope of the *Jencks* decision.[14]

For the most part, Hoover attempted to keep the FBI out of the political arena. The Bureau's efforts to effect a change in the law were carried on in a silent and subtle campaign within the confines of Congress. Yet silent and subtle as it was, Representative Emmanuel Celler (D. N.Y.) felt forced to reprimand the Bureau for being over-zealous. Celler argued on the House floor that " a whole hullabaloo has been made over this situation. There is nothing in here [*Jencks* case] concerning national security, but there are emanating... from the FBI great waves of propaganda that indicate [a situation] to the contrary...."[15] Celler noted that the FBI was a "non-political entity and should not exert pressure on members or through the press. I hope," he concluded, "the FBI will not again indulge in the vast prop-aganda that has been generated to support this bill."[16]

Before August, 1957, Hoover had only indirectly alluded to the need to rectify the Court's holding in the *Jencks* case. After that date, he apparently felt compelled to lend his full support to the campaign. He did this by writing a letter to Representative Joe Martin (R. Mass.) giving his unqualified support. With respect to the pending legislation, Hoover said that "its enactment is vital to the future ability of the Federal Bureau of Investigation to carry out its internal security and law enforcement responsibilities."[17] He further commented:

> Since the *Jencks* decision...we have faced one obstacle after another...sources of information have been closed to our agents because of the fear that the confidence we could once guarantee could no longer be assured. We also have experienced a reluc-tance on the part of numerous citizens to cooperate as freely as they once did.[18]

The lobbying campaign carried on by the FBI proved to be quite effective, for the only piece of anti-Court legislation which Congress passed was the *Jencks* bill, which the Bureau so strongly supported.

The key to understanding the disagreement here is the fact that the *Mallory* and *Jencks* decisions impeded the free exercise of law enforcement functions. It appears that the agencies did not have the concept of the ideal law enforcement program, requiring that every protection be extended to those unpopular citizens who are suspect. In any event, the agencies undoubtedly agreed with George L. Hart, Jr., of the Washington Council on Law Enforcement, who stated that the *Mallory* and *Jencks* decisions threw the "balance of interest out of balance" in favor of the individual over the public.[19]

EBBING OF DISCONTENT

The vocal discontent of law enforcement officials with the Court's opinions in *Mallory* and *Jencks* began to ebb after a few years. The conflict was renewed, however, in the early sixties when the High

Tribunal began another series of decisions concerning state and local law enforcement officials. These decisions have had such a major impact upon law enforcement practices that they require comment. Furthermore, the development of the law in this area stimulated another round of political combat between the judiciary and the various enforcement agencies.

SEARCH AND SEIZURE

The first decision to renew the fray was *Mapp v. Ohio*,[20] a case concerned with the Fourth Amendment's protection against unreasonable search and seizure. While the Fourth Amendment had been read into the due process clause of the Fourteenth Amendment in *Wolf v. Colorado*,[21] (and thus made applicable to the states), the justices did not require the states to adopt what is known as the federal exclusionary rule. This rule, announced in *Weeks v. United States*,[22] states that illegally seized evidence cannot be used in a federal criminal proceeding. In the *Weeks'* case, the Court reasoned that the adoption of an exclusionary rule was the only effective way of enforcing the guarantee against unreasonable search and seizure. In the 1941 *Wolf* decision, Justice Frankfurter, speaking for the majority of the Court, concluded that the states could decide for themselves as to the best method of protection against search and seizures. States could also utilize civil actions against law enforcement officers or criminal prosecutions to enforce the Fourth Amendment guarantee. In any event, it was the prerogative of the states to choose the device.

REVOLUTION BEGINS

The *Mapp* decision in 1961 not only changed the law with respect to the exclusionary rule, but also signaled the beginning of what has been referred to as a "Constitutional revolution" in the area of criminal law. The facts in *Mapp* are quite complex. Briefly, three Cleveland policemen went to the residence of Doll Ree Mapp on the basis of information that a person wanted by the police for questioning was hiding in her home. After several attempts to get into the house, the police forced their way in through an outer door. They handed Mrs. Mapp a piece of paper which purported to be a search warrant (but was in fact not a warrant) and proceeded to search the premises. The search uncovered a number of lewd pictures which were seized by the police. Mrs. Mapp was convicted on the basis of the seized evidence which the court later defined as illegally seized because the police could not produce a search warrant.

In delivering the majority opinion for the Court, Justice Clark concluded that the arguments which had been used to support limiting the exclusionary rule to the federal government in the *Wolf* case were no longer meaningful. Clark reasoned that nothing can destroy a government more quickly than its failure "to observe its own laws, or worse, its disregard of the charter of its own existence." In view of this, the Court extended the exclusionary rule making it an essential part of the due process clause of the Fourteenth Amendment, and leaving the states no longer free to choose their method for guaranteeing protection against unreasonable search and seizures.

The *Mapp* decision had a far-reaching effect upon state law enforcement practices. Evidence which had been acceptable in state criminal proceedings was no longer admissible. The obvious result was to place significant limitations upon certain police practices — limitations not welcomed by many law enforcement agencies. Further complicating the situation was the Court's ruling in *Ker v. California.*[23] In this case the Court held that the states were subject to the same Constitutional standards as the federal government in prohibiting unreasonable search and seizures. Since the federal standards were in most cases more rigid than those found in the several states, this in itself placed a significant limitation on state and local law enforcement officials.

Another major case which significantly concerned law enforcement dealt with right to counsel. In 1963, in *Gideon v. Wainwright,*[24] the Supreme Court read the Sixth Amendment guarantee of right to counsel into the due process clause of the Fourteenth Amendment. Actually many commentators had felt that the right to counsel was made applicable to the states in *Powell v. Alabama,*[25] a decision dating from 1932. But in subsequent cases, especially *Betts v. Brady,*[26] the Court made clear that the states had to guarantee an accused right to counsel only in capital cases or where a defendant for some reason was placed at a disadvantage because of lack of counsel. Justice Roberts, in delivering the majority opinion in *Betts,* reasoned that, historically, right to counsel was not fundamental to a fair hearing in *all* criminal cases. As stated by Justice Cardozo, before a provision of the Bill of Rights can be read into the due process clause of the Fourteenth Amendment, it must be of "the very essence of a scheme of ordered liberty."[27]

REVIEW OF RIGHT TO COUNSEL

By 1963, the Court decided it was time to review its thinking on the right to counsel, and *Gideon v. Wainwright* provided an opportunity. For the reader who wishes to study this issue in depth, Anthony Lewis has written a fine study of the right to counsel cases in *Gideon's*

Trumpet published in 1964.[28] Here it suffices to note that Clarence Gideon was tried and convicted of breaking into and stealing goods from a pool hall. At his trial, Gideon requested the Florida court to provide him with an attorney, since he was an indigent person. This was refused since under the state law the court could appoint counsel only in capital cases. Gideon defended himself at the proceeding. He made an opening statement, cross-examined witnesses, put on his own witnesses, made a short concluding statement protesting his innocence. He was found guilty and sentenced to prison. While confined, Gideon petitioned the Supreme Court in *forma pauperis* for a review of his case. The Supreme Court granted *certiorari* in order to clarify the law with respect to the right to counsel guarantee.

BETTS DECISION OVERRULED

Justice Black, in delivering the unanimous opinion of the Court, overruled the philosophy of the *Betts* decision. Black reasoned that the Court's position in *Betts v. Brady* was really a departure from the law as announced in *Powell v. Alabama*. In *Gideon* the Court was bringing the right to counsel cases back into their proper Constitutional perspective. Stressing the ideas of Justice Sutherland in the *Powell* case, Black noted that even "the intelligent and educated layman has small and sometimes no skill in the science of the law." At any rate, in 1963 the Sixth Amendment guarantee to right to counsel became implicit in the "ordered concept of liberty." The due process clause of the Fourteenth Amendment now required the states to guarantee defendants right to counsel in criminal cases.

Taken by itself the *Gideon* case probably did not cause too much alarm in law enforcement circles. Only three states (including Florida) submitted briefs arguing for preservation of the *Betts* decision. Twenty-two states argued that *Betts* was "an anachronism when handed down, and should be overruled." The real problem evinced itself in the case's after-effects. Since the decision was held to be retroactive, a number of inmates who had been sent to prison without the benefit of counsel were released. More importantly, and of greater concern to law enforcement officials, was the question of when the right to counsel was to begin. Was it to apply only in the courtroom, upon arraignment, or would it be extended to the interrogation room of the jail-house?

It was not long before the Court was confronted by this difficult question. In 1964, two extremely controversial cases were handed down by the High Tribunal — *Massiah v. United States*[29] and *Escobedo v. Illinois*.[30] While both cases shed some light on the issue, the cases seemed to provide more questions than answers.

Massiah, arrested and arraigned on a narcotics charge, retained an attorney and was released on bail. Government agents arranged with Massiah's co-defendant to install a radio transmitter under the front seat of the co-defendant's automobile. Later, a federal officer was able to obtain by means of the radio transmitter incriminating statements from a conversation between Massiah and the co-defendant. This incriminating evidence was testified to by the federal officer at Massiah's trail and Massiah was convicted.

Justice Stewart, in speaking for the majority of the Court, reversed Massiah's conviction. Stewart cited *Powell v. Alabama* to support the majority's position. In *Powell* the Court had noted that:

> ...during the most critical period of the proceedings...that is to say from the time of their arraignment until the beginning of their trial, when consultation, thoroughgoing investigation and preparation [are] vitally important, the defendants...[are] as much entitled to such aid [of counsel] during that period as at the trial itself.[31]

Since Massiah had already been arraigned and had a lawyer, the Court was not left with much choice in this case. But from a law enforcement standpoint, the *Massiah* decision restricted officers in the continuation of their investigation and securing of evidence after arraignment. Even more perplexing to law enforcement officers than the *Massiah* decision was the opinion rendered by the Court in *Escobedo v. Illinois*.

Danny Escobedo was arrested without a warrant and interrogated in connection with his brother-in-law's murder. He made no statement at that time and was released pursuant to a writ of habeas corpus which had been secured by his attorney. Approximately ten days later, Benedict DiGerlando, later indicted with Escobedo for the murder, told the police that Danny had fired the fatal shots. Danny Escobedo and his sister were arrested and taken to police headquarters. Escobedo asked repeatedly to see his lawyer during the interrogation at the jailhouse, and simultaneously the lawyer was in the next room demanding to see his client, but they never got together. Additional evidence produced at the trial indicated that a police officer who knew Escobedo had told Danny that if he would pin the rap on DiGerlando, he could go home and would only have to act as a witness in the case. On the basis of this assurance, Escobedo implicated himself in the murder by saying that DiGerlando had shot his brother-in-law.

The legal issue with which the Supreme Court had to wrestle pertained not to the issue of right to counsel per se, but the question of the stage of criminal investigation at which a person is guaranteed this right. Justice Black delivered the opinion for the majority, and was joined by Warren, Brennan, Douglas, and Goldberg. White, Har-

lan, Stewart, and Clark all dissented. Black reasoned that it was irrele-
vent that Escobedo had not yet been indicted. Once the investigation
ceases to be a general inquiry into an unresolved crime and begins to
focus on a particular suspect who has been taken into custody, at this
point the accused has a Constitutional right to counsel. Black went on
to note that the right to counsel "would indeed be hollow if it began at
a period when few confessions were obtained." Speaking in terms of
the philosophy which seems to permeate the so-called liberal opinions
of the Court's majority bloc, he said, "Our Constitution, unlike some
others, strikes the balance in favor of the right of the accused. . . ."

OPINIONS OF THREE DISSENTERS

Justices Harlan, Stewart, and 'White all wrote separate dissenting
opinions. Three objections seem to stand out. First, there was the feeling that the *Escobedo* case would not be limited to its facts, thus providing guidelines in future decisions. Second, the rule extending the right
to counsel guarantee beyond the judicial stage of a prosecution would
hamper criminal investigation. And finally the dissenting judges, in
particularly Justice White, felt that the Court in effect was creating a
new test for the admissibility of confessions. Heretofore confessions
were admissible on the basis of their being voluntarily or involuntarily
obtained. But under the *Escobedo* interpretation, a confession voluntarily obtained could be omitted from evidence if secured without the
benefit of counsel, and if the proceedings had moved from the investi-
gatory to the accusatory stage. In fact, when the essentials are examined, it does indeed appear that the right to counsel guarantee begins
when the interrogation passes from the first to the second of these
stages.

The alleged vagueness of the *Escobedo* test, coupled with the
dissenting opinions, caused considerable alarm in law enforcement
circles. Immediate reaction tended toward the emotional. Garrett
Byrne, President of the National Association of District Attorneys, remarked that if five men sat down to think carefully how to destroy the
country they could not have done more harm to law enforcement than
the present Supreme Court majority.[32] Former New York Police Com-
missioner Michael Murphy criticized the Court for a "series of decisions on confessions and searches and seizures which unduly hampered
law enforcement." "What the Court is doing," Murphy noted, "is akin
to requiring one boxer to fight by Marquis of Queensbury rules while
permitting the other to butt, gouge, and bite."[33]

Doubtless *Escobedo* did create confusion not only for law enforcement people, but for the lower courts as well. Some judges interpreted
Escobedo as narrowly limiting the case to its facts. Others took a broad-

er view of the decision, interpreting it as requiring law enforcement officers to apprise an accused of his right to counsel as well as of the fact that anything the suspect said could be used against him.

The so-called Constitutional revolution in criminal law did not come to an end with the *Escobedo* decision. In 1964, there were significant Constitutional changes with respect to the Fifth Amendment guarantee against self-incrimination as well. For many years the Supreme Court had held that the privilege against self-incrimination was not sufficiently fundamental to a scheme of ordered liberty to be read into the due process clause of the Fourteenth Amendment.[34] But in *Malloy v. Hogan*,[35] the Court reconsidered its position and by a 5-4 vote read the privilege into the due process clause. This shift of position was harmonious with the recent inclination of the High Tribunal to include selectively in the Fourteenth Amendment most of the fundamental guarantees of the Bill of Rights (which initially was directed only at the federal government.) Here again the effect has been to restrict the states in their law enforcement functions.

The Court in favoring individual liberties over the more flexible law enforcement practices continued in 1965. This was pointed up by two cases in particular — *Pointer v. Texas*[36] (dealing with the Sixth Amendment right of confrontation) and *Griffin v. California*[37] (dealing with the Fifth Amendment privilege against self-incrimination and the "comment rule"). Both underlined the legal trend toward favoring individual rights.

CLIMAX OF REVOLUTION

The Constitutional revolution in the area of law enforcement may have reached its climax in June, 1966. At this time, the Supreme Court handed down the long-awaited right-to-counsel cases which supposedly were to clarify the *Escobedo* decision. But where the *Escobedo* decision revolved around the Sixth Amendment right to counsel, the new series of cases focused on the Fifth Amendment privilege against self-incrimination. Actually it could be reasoned that the two provisions were linked together in order to protect the accused against invalid interrogation.

These four controversial decisions, which undoubtedly will shape the future of police interrogation procedures, have been conveniently named the *Miranda* decisions, because the first was labelled *Miranda v. Arizona*.[38] In each of the four, a suspect was arrested and interrogated. While in custody, and in the course of interrogation, each suspect confessed to the crime of which he had been accused. There was no evidence in any of the cases to show that the suspects had been warned of their Constitutional rights. Each was convicted on the basis of his confession.

In a 5-4 decision the Supreme Court reversed each of the lower court cases.[39] Chief Justice Warren delivered the majority opinion for the Court. Since the *Massiah* and *Escobedo* cases had created a good deal of spirited debate in legal circles, Warren took this occasion to use *Miranda* as a resolution of this conflict. In the process, he developed a number of new rules which limit the power of law enforcement in interrogating witnesses. Having undertaken what he referred to as a thorough examination of the *Escobedo* philosophy, the Chief Justice reaffirmed the underlying concepts. He then proceeded to extend the *Escobedo* doctrine to what appeared to be the next logical step in protecting an accused who has been taken into custody by the police — the requirement that an accused must be warned of his Constitutional rights before the police may interrogate the suspect in custody.

The majority opinion concluded that "the prosecution may not use statements, whether exculpatory or inculpatory, stemming from custodial interrogation of the defendant unless it demonstrates the use of procedural safeguards effective to secure the privilege against self-incrimination."[40] Custodial interrogation, the Court defined as the period when "a person had been taken into custody or otherwise deprived of his freedom of action in any significant way." In essence, this means that confessions and other incriminating evidence may not be used in a criminal proceeding if the suspect is within the custody of the police or is deprived of his freedom in a significant way, and has not been afforded his Constitutional safeguards. The next question of course is what constitutes these Constitutional safeguards.

WARNINGS TO ACCUSED

Chief Justice Warren was quite precise as to what these procedural safeguards entailed. An accused must be given four specific warnings by the police:

1. He must be warned that he has a right to remain silent.
2. He must be warned that any statement he makes may be used against him.
3. He must be warned that he has a right to have counsel present during the interrogation.
4. He must be warned that if he cannot afford counsel, an attorney will be appointed for him.

These warnings, which by themselves will significantly change law enforcement practices in a number of states, constituted only the beginning of the Court's opinion. Further rules supplementing these pre-interrogation warnings and protecting the rights of the accused under the Fifth Amendment are spelled out by the majority. Warren proceeded to note that an accused may voluntarily, intelligently, and knowingly waive these rights. However, the burden rests with the prosecution to demonstrate at the trial that the rights were waived under these conditions. In addition, at any time during the interrogation an accused may indicate that he wants to consult with an attorney before proceeding further. Finally, whenever an accused is alone and in any manner indicates that he does not wish to be interrogated, the police may not question him.[41]

The majority concluded that all four cases before the Court "share the same salient features — incommunicado interrogation of individuals in a police-dominated atmosphere, resulting in self-incriminating statements without full warnings of constitutional rights."[42] All four convictions were thrown out.

As to the theoretical basis of the majority philosophy here, Warren cited a number of texts and manuals documenting the techniques which police use in breaking down a suspect. "The entire thrust of police interrogation . . . [is] to put the defendant in such an emotional state as to impair his capacity for rational judgment."[43]

He noted that a person who is in police custody cannot be otherwise than under compulsion to speak. He quoted *Malloy v. Hogan* to point out that the underlying assumption of the Fifth Amendment is to guarantee an accused the right "to remain silent unless he chooses to speak in the unfettered exercise of his own will."[44]

In conclusion Warren stated that the rules applied in the *Miranda* decisions are not as novel as many would lead us to believe. The Federal Bureau of Investigation to a large extent has incorporated these ideas in its law enforcement practices for some time, and countries such as England, Scotland, India and Ceylon, as well as the U.S. Armed Forces via the United States Code of Military Justice have substantially followed the same practices. Certain ones, however, such as the requirement for presence of an attorney before interrogation can commence, are not necessarily included by these agencies and nations.

Four justices dissented in the *Miranda* decision — Clark, White, Harlan, and Stewart, and each wrote a separate opinion. They agreed that the majority was going too far too fast, and that the traditional approach to the admissibility of confessions in a criminal proceeding was more than sufficient to deal with the problem of protecting individual rights. In addition, not only were confessions inadmissible if physically or psychologically obtained, but the Court over the years had developed a test looking to the "totality of the circumstances" of each case to make sure that due process of law had not been violated.[45] Justice White noted that only *compelled* testimony is proscribed by the Fifth Amendment. In voluntary confession there is no compulsion.

EMOTIONALISM APPARENT

The emotional atmosphere surrounding the *Miranda* decisions is apparent in the three dissenting opinions, each of which hit hard at the majority. Justice Clark argued that such a "strict Constitutional specific inserted at the nerve center of crime detection may well kill the patient."[46] Justice White, admitting that the Court could make new law under certain circumstances, reasoned that such judicial legislation should not be made on mere speculation alone, but upon sound authority which he was unable to find in the majority opinion. There was every reason to believe, he continued, that many criminals who would have been convicted on what "this Court thought to be the most satisfactory kind of evidence, will now under this new version of the Fifth Amendment, either not be tried at all or acquitted if the State's evidence, minus the confession, is put to the test of litigation."[47] The decision of the Court could very well "return a killer, a rapist or other criminal to the streets and to the environment which produced him, to repeat his crime whenever it pleases him."[48]

Harlan's opinion was perhaps the most critical. He began with the statement: "I believe the decision of the Court represents poor Constitutional law and entails harmful consequences for the country at large."[49] He felt that support of the majority position required "a strained reading of history and precedent and a disregard of the very pragmatic concerns that alone may on occasion justify such strains." In stressing the risk to society, he reasoned that the "social costs of crime are too great to call the new rules anything but a hazardous experimentation."[50] Questioning the theoretical as well as practical wisdom of Warren's decision, Harlan continued to emphasize that the Court had failed to demonstrate through legal history of libertarian philosophy that these new rules were desirable in the context of our society. He felt that ". . . to provide counsel for the suspect during interrogation simply invites the end of interrogation." In this concluding paragraph, Harlan argued that "Nothing in the letter or the spirit of the Constitution or in the precedents squares with the heavy-handed and one-sided action that is so precipitously taken by the Court. . . . This Court is forever adding new stories to the temples of Constitutional law, and the temples have a way of collapsing when one story too many is added."[51]

OPINIONS DIFFER

In the final anaylsis the differences between the majority and minority opinions seemed to be twofold. The first revolved around a commitment to individual liberty. The majority view elevated individual rights to a pre-eminent position guarding them jealously against governmental encroachment. The minority view, in attempting to strike a balance between civil liberties and public security, felt in this case that the pendulum should be swung to the side of law enforcement. It was the minority view that individual rights could be adequately protected without placing "warning" restrictions upon the police. The second basis of separation was more technical, pertaining to the view each side has of custodial interrogation. Chief Justice Warren held that incommunicado interrogation in a police-dominated atmosphere has a *compelling* affect upon criminal suspect and is thus repugnant to the Fifth Amendment privilege against self-incrimination. The dissenting judges held that custodial interrogation by the police is not compulsion *per se*. Indeed, compulsion can only be ascertained by the "totality of circumstances" surrounding each case, depending primarily on the factors of physical and psychological coercion.

The fundamental conflict in the *Miranda* decisions was perhaps the most significant since legislative re-apportionment. The philosophical supports of both sides are reasonable and sound, and since these decisions have changed law enforcement practices in many jurisdictions, a debate is almost certain to continue for many years.

REACTIONS OF OFFICIALS

Law enforcement officials reacted to the *Miranda* decisions in four separate ways — first with a note of caution. Most officials did not have access to the Court's opinions and waited for precise information before commenting. As a result of erroneous news reports, critics of the Court expressing premature reactions had been stigmatized in the past and as a result they came forth with a guarded response.

Statements of firm disapproval were a second type of reaction, but this ideological dissent was coupled with the attitude that law enforcement officials would simply have to live with the decision. Illustrative of this was the response of Chief Phillip Purcell, president of the International Association of Chiefs of Police and head of the Newton, Massachusetts, Police Department. "I wholeheartedly concur with the dissenting justices.. [but] we will have to go along with the limitations, such as they are." [52]

The third type of response was equally mild. This reaction, though not praising the Court's opinion, acknowledged that the new rules of law would not significantly affect existing progressive law enforcement practices. District Attorney Isidore Dollinger of the Bronx, New York, noted that the decisions appeared to require "exactly what we are doing already."[53] Police Chief Harold Dill of Denver was quoted as saying: "They make a big thing of confessions, but if you don't have any evidence you can't convict anyone anyway. This decision won't change things with our department and we've had a pretty good record of convictions...."[54] California's Attorney General Thomas Lynch noted that with the exception of the lawyer requirement, the same rules were already implemented by California State peace officers. And Bernard L. Garmire — Chief of the Tucson, Arizona, police — acknowledged that the law enforcement practices of his department were not out of line with the decision.

MORE CRITICAL RESPONSE

Closely associated with this type of response but somewhat more critical were the comments of County Attorney William J. Schafer III of Pima County, Arizona. Schafer, an able and well known young prosecutor, stipulated that *Miranda* caused very little change in their procedures. His office already warned prospective in-custody defendants of their rights. He went on to criticize, however, the majority judges for failure to realize fully the practical consequences of their decision. "Many cases can now never be made. Confessions or admissions are absolutely essential to a great many cases. This seems to be especially true in murder cases. Since *Escobedo,* many of these have not been brought to trial because of the lack of an admissible confession. Police can sharpen their investigative tools all they want, but they can't manufacture a fingerprint."[55]

The fourth type of reaction to the *Miranda* decisions was highly critical. Typical of this response was the attitude of Assistant Police Chief George Seber, of Houston, Texas. Seber noted that the police "will be greatly hindered in solving crimes where there have been no witnesses. You might as well burn up the books on the science of police interrogation."[56] Henry C. Ashley of Garland, Texas, said that this was the "Damnedest thing I ever heard of.... We may as well close up shop." In Reno, Nevada, Sheriff C. W. Young argued that it's "getting to the point where we can't even use a confession if a person wants to confess." Police Chief Noel A. Jones noted that the *Miranda* decisions constituted "another shackle that the Supreme Court gives us from time to time in the handling of criminal cases. Some day they may give us an equal chance with the criminals." Detective Inspector W. R. Bland of Tampa, Florida, said that in his opinion, the Court's ruling would further tie the hands of the police. Duane R. Nedrud, executive director of the National District Attorneys Association, reasoned that these decisions not only hamper law enforcement, but to some extent place a stigma on the already poor public image which the police possess. "If the Court wants [to ban police interrogation]" Nedrud concluded, "this is the court's prerogative and right, but it can't say to police: 'Solve crimes in some other way,' when in effect they can't."[57]

ADJUSTMENTS BEGINNING

It is still early to judge the impact of the *Miranda* case upon law enforcement practices. Apparently some police departments are already living fairly comfortably with the rules as handed down by the Court. Others are not sure they can adjust. Indeed, attempts may be made in the future to change the right-to-counsel and self-incrimination policies as handed down by the Court. Efforts to accomplish this in the past, however, with the exception of the Jencks Act, have been conspicuously unsuccessful. Still, within a month after the *Miranda* decisions were handed down, a regional convention of the International Chiefs of Police called for a national study group to examine the recent decisions of the Supreme Court relating to search and seizure, and the questioning of suspects. The grounds for a continuing battle between certain segments of law enforcement and the Court seem to be firmly established.

Tempering the criticism of the Court, though perhaps only temporarily, in *Johnson v. New Jersey*, the Supreme Court held that the *Miranda* decisions would not be applied retroactively.[58]

It is not difficult to see why law enforcement officers have evidenced a good deal of concern over the trend of Supreme Court decisions which placed significant restrictions upon the police, restrictions allegedly making the law enforcement function more difficult. Because of this, most of the criticism from law enforcement circles has been predicated upon "decisional obstruction." While it is clear that the police widely differ with the social philosophy emanating from the Court, their main concern has been with removing the barriers which the Court's decisions supposedly have placed upon them.

A recent article in one of the nation's leading newspapers surveyed a number of law enforcement officials to gauge their reaction to the Court's decisions over the past few years.[59] Colonel Stanley Schrotel, Cincinnati's police chief, stated that "these rulings have taken from the police the tools that are essential to do an effective investigative job." Orlando Wilson, Chicago's reform police superintendent, noted that we simply "cannot live with their recent decisions." Denver Police Chief Harold A. Dill reasoned that "our laws are all right. Interpretation is poor." Robert Gaynor Berry, criminal prosecutor from Reno, Nevada,

posed the question whether "individual rights are really being protected in this society...[or] whether criminal rights are actually being
protected to the detriment of the innocent people of this country." The
then Chief Parker of the Los Angeles Police force strongly criticized
the Court for the restrictions placed upon police authority. He felt that
the trend of decisions had tragically weakened the police establishment
and urged law enforcement officials to speak out more energetically.

J. Edgar Hoover, who occasionally has made statements critical of
the Supreme Court's attitude toward law enforcement, has been quoted
as saying:

> We are faced today with one of the most disturbing trends I have
> witnessed in my years of law enforcement; an overzealous pity
> for the criminal and an equivalent disregard for his victim.[60]

Fred Sondern, Jr., in writing an article for a popular magazine entitled
"Take the Handcuffs Off Our Police," has argued that in the 1950's the
legal pendulum had swung too far in the area of police reform.[61] Even
judges have become concerned. J. Edward Lumbard, Federal Court of
Appeals judge, has noted that the "questioning and detention of suspects has become a no man's land, which, for the most part, is unchart-
ed and for which there are today no reliable guides."[62] Chief Justice
Bell of the Pennsylvania Supreme Court, in evidencing his concern
with disrespect for law and order, felt that one of the most important
factors contributing to this disrespect was the "unrealistic judges."[63]

Judge John F. Scileppi of New York, in a 1964 article entitled "Is
Society Shortchanged at the Bar of Justice?" also joined the judicial
critics. In commenting on the *Mapp* decision, Judge Scileppi suggested
that there may be an imbalance in the law. "The Bill of Rights protects
the guilty, but what about the rights of the rest of society?" He urged
the courts to stop bending over backward to give the defendant added
protection.[64]

During the 1964 Presidential campaign, Candidate Barry Goldwater acted as a political spokesman for law enforcement critics. If
elected President, Goldwater pledged to work to overturn the recent
Supreme Court decisions which had invaded the province of state law
enforcement. He argued that criminals were being needlessly pam-
pered and that law and order were being sacrificed "just to give
criminals a sporting chance to go free."[65] Goldwater pledged that upon
election to the Presidency, he would work to abolish the *Mallory* rule,
give the states back their power to prosecute criminals and appoint
Supreme Court justices whose views on law enforcement would be
sympathetic.

LAW ENFORCEMENT DEBATE

A significant insight into the Court's attitude toward the Constitution and its relationship to law enforcement comes from a debate waged between Fred Inbau of Northwestern Law School and Yale Kamisar of Minnesota Law School. Professor Inbau has consistently been the outstanding academic spokesman defending law enforcement practices. Professor Kamisar on the other hand, has been the champion defender of the Supreme Court. This series of exchanges occurred in 1962 in the *Journal of Criminal Law, Criminology, and Police Science.* Professor Inbau began the discussion with an article entitled "Public Safety v. Individual Civil Liberties: The Prosecutor's Stand."[66] The article actually originated as an address to the National District Attorneys' Association held in Portland, Oregon, 1961. The basic theme of Inbau's argument was that the Court had assumed a dangerous attitude toward law enforcement with its "turn 'em loose" decisions. "The Court has taken it upon itself without Constitutional authority, to police the police."[67] While Inbau reasoned that he was not opposed to the Bill of Rights, he felt more attention should be placed on the Preamble to the Constitution with its references to domestic tranquility and the public welfare. In his address Inbau discussed some of the decisions most perplexing to law enforcement — in particular *Mallory* and *Mapp,* which he regarded as typical of the Court's attempt to police the police. "Law enforcement officers cannot offer the required protection demanded of them from within the straitjacket placed upon them by the present Court...."[68]

Professor Kamisar's rejoinder was largely a careful analysis of the Supreme Court's position in a number of the cases to which Professor Inbau had addressed himself.[69] Kamisar attempted to demonstrate that the Court had not made an abrupt change in the law, but that the law had evolved slowly. The *Mallory* case was nothing more than an extension of *McNabb v. United States,*[70] which had been rendered fourteen years before. The philosophy of the *Mapp* decision, though admittedly applied to the states for the first time, could be traced back to 1914 when the Court first promulgated the exclusionary rule in *Weeks v. United States.*[71] Although he responded to the case analyses point by point, Kamisar was somewhat more concerned with Inbau's view of the Supreme Court's function. Kamisar noted that it is "one thing to differ with the Court about what the law is or ought to be; it is quite another thing to deny that the Court has the power or the right to say what the law is."[72] The overall problem, according to Kamisar, should not be couched in terms of "policing the police" as Inbau had phrased it; rather, it should be looked upon as "enforcing the Constitution."

DISPUTES CRYSTALLIZED

The debate served to identify and crystallize some of the major disputes between the law enforcement critics and the defenders of the Court. Many decisions rendered by the Court since that time have perpetuated the disagreement which shows signs of continuing in years to come. The effect in the main has been healthy, providing the Court with a continual challenge to keep its decisions abreast of the times. In addition to the Inbau-Kamisar exchange, a wealth of articles has appeared in law reviews and other academic journals. These on the whole are substantive, dealing with the legalities of the controversy, and seldom contain political criticism directed toward the Court.

Although much of the comment on the Court's recent controversial decisions have been devoid of emotionalism, the few conspicuous exceptions have been a matter of concern to some of the Court's personnel. In 1963, in an address to the Aspen Institute for Humanistic Studies, Justice Brennan commented on some of these attacks.[73] He noted that the Court's survival is threatened by criticism based on a lack of understanding. While Brennan was primarily concerned with the immediate reaction to the School Prayer case, he alluded also to certain decisions affecting law enforcement practices. "Those who opposed the Court," Brennan noted, "should at least read the decision to find out how it was made." This admonition, while less applicable to law enforcement officials than other critics, was aimed at all those persons who become disturbed with a particular decision and react emotionally before looking into the delicate task confronting the justices. No case brought before the Supreme Court is an easy one, for if it were, the issue would have been resolved by one of the lower courts. Therefore, each case demands delicate balancing of the issue of individual liberties against the problems of public order. Whatever the outcome, it is certain the justices do not undertake their obligation lightly.

There is increasing evidence of late that most law enforcement officers are recognizing that regardless of disagreement with the decisions they must work within the system. H. Alan Long in 1965 reasoned in *The Police Chief*, the official publication of the International Association of Chiefs of Police, that law enforcement officers must live with the development of the law[74] and that the way to temper the trend of Court opinions is through better and more effective law enforcement. Indeed, Captain Raymond H. McConnell (head of the detective division of the Michigan State Police) suggests that the trend of the Court's decisions is partly the result of faulty police work.[75] Chief Curtis Brostron, of the St. Louis police force, has noted that since the recent decisions involving law enforcement make the job of the police more difficult, the police "must become better, more professional officers to get the job done."[76]

The attitude of working within the framework of the law was evidenced also at the 1965 annual convention of the International Association of Chiefs of Police. Rather than spending time in criticism, the I.A.C.P. passed a resolution instructing the Executive Director to prepare and disseminate to the extent possible all material regarding the Court's decision so that officers could better know and understand the law of the land.[77] The same attitude was shown in the new prearraignment code drafted by the American Law Institute. Financed by the Ford Foundation, the code was drawn up by forty judges, law professors, policemen, and prosecutors with considerable expertise. The code, which may serve as a model for all states to follow, attempts to spell out clearly and precisely what a police officer can and cannot do from the time of apprehension until the accused is arraigned before a judge.

There are several other benefits to society from the controversial Supreme Court decisions in the area of criminal law. The *Gideon* case, for instance, initiated extensive discussion on the need for public defender offices. Such offices have since been instituted in a number of metropolitan areas in order to cope with the increased demand by indigents for counsel.

Furthermore, the training of law enforcement officers is becoming increasingly sophisticated, not only with respect to the traditional functions, but also in the trainees' orientation to the development of the law. Great emphasis is being placed on apprising police of the steps which must be taken to avoid losing a case due to ignorance of the law. As an example of the trend of current police education, a 1965 training bulletin used by the Tucson, Arizona, police force deals with the problem of confessions as follows: "When an investigation shifts from a general inquiry of facts and begins to focus upon a particular person as a suspect, this person must be advised of his rights prior to an interrogation or an attempt to gain a confession."[78] This philosophy is taken almost directly from the *Escobedo* decision. The bulletin then instructs the trainee as to the steps he must take in advising an accused of his rights.

1. The subject *must* be advised of [the officer's] identity and authority.
2. The subject *must* be advised of his right to speak to an attorney before speaking to the police.
3. The subject *must* be advised that he does not have to say anything.
4. The subject *must* be advised that anything he might say may be used against him.

All of this points to the fact that law enforcement officials are working to adjust their practices to conform with recent Supreme Court decisions. This work has the ultimate goal of maximum protection for the accused, to be achieved in a context of law enforcement and public security.

7. THE PROFESSIONAL CRITICS

While Congressmen and a wide variety of interest-group critics have captured newspaper headlines with loud attacks on the Supreme Court, a smaller group of professional critics has been similarly but less vocally engaged. This select group, composed principally of judges, bar associations, and academicians, for the most part has not sought national attention. Indeed these critics have attempted to avoid partisan politics and newspaper headlines, and preoccupied themselves with the more sophisticated and intimate problems of the judicial process today.

The interest of these critics has not been focused exclusively on problems of legal methodology, however. A rather tight-knit minority within this professional group has emulated the so-called result-oriented critics in manifesting lack of accord with the trend of recent Supreme Court decisions. In fact, the emotional and irrational overtones earlier identified with the result-oriented school of non-professionals is characteristic also of this handful of professional critics.

The first group of professional critics which requires consideration are the judges themselves. In 1956, former Supreme Court Justice James Byrnes wrote a biting article for *U.S. News and World Report* entitled "The Supreme Court Must Be Curbed."[1] In chastising the High Bench for its holding in the School Segregation cases, Byrnes gave an air of respectability to the vitriolic attacks emanating from dissident Southern Congressmen. According to Byrnes, the Court did not interpret the Constitution in *Brown v. Board of Education*; rather, the High Tribunal amended it. With this as a theme, Byrnes attacked the sociological and psychological basis of the *Brown* decision. Byrnes also attempted to impugn the credibility of Gunnar Myrdal — one of the authorities cited by the Court — and several of Myrdal's associates.

In particular, Dr. K. B. Clark was attacked because he had worked for NAACP, and E. Franklin Frazier because of his testimony before a House Un-American Activities Committee, which supposedly revealed that he had been connected with several Communist causes. This attack again was the "guilt-by-association" tactic practiced so frequently by other Southern critics of the School Segregation decisions. The former justice concluded his article by reasoning that "Power intoxicates men. It is never voluntarily surrendered. It must be taken from them. The Supreme Court must be curbed."[2]

The Byrnes article was just the beginning of a number of political assaults by the former justice. He became the most respected critic of all in the eyes of the conservative Southerners, and went on speaking engagements to review the more controversial decisions and stress his central theme that the Court must be curbed.[3]

DISTURBED BY IDEOLOGY

The real motivation for Byrnes' criticism, however, was not the decision-making process (though he claimed this to be so). The former justice was concerned with results, and though he perpetually condemned the Court for overt judicial activism, it was really the liberal ideology that disturbed him. Professor Wallace Mendelson in an article entitled "The Court Must Not Be Curbed: A Reply to Mr. Byrnes,"[4] cites numerous cases in which Byrnes as a justice behaved in the same "judicially active" manner for which he criticized the present Court. In *Edwards v. California* Byrnes did not let what the Court had decided in 1936 stand in the way of his belief in 1941.[5] "We do not consider ourselves bound by the language referred to [in 1936]" stated the former justice. Yet Byrnes criticized Chief Justice Warren for not considering himself bound by the Court's 1896 philosophy upon the basis of which *Plessy v. Ferguson* (the separate but equal doctrine) was decided.

There were many other examples of judges criticizing the Court. William Old, an appellate judge from Chesterfield County, Virginia, felt that the recent decisions of the Supreme Court were so revolutionary in nature that the Court must be stripped of some of its appellate jurisdiction.[6] Old testified thus in supporting the passage of the Jenner bill in 1958. Judge Walter Jones, writing in the *Montgomery Advertiser*, felt that the Court was tearing down the Constitution and building in Washington a "tyrannically dictatorial" government which was steadily destroying all local self-government.[7] To rectify this trend, Judge Jones suggested the Supreme Court justices be selected by (1) the highest courts of the states, (2) patriotic organizations, (3) state bar associations, or (4) state governors. Since all of the above categories are more or less conservative in character, appointees selected by the above goups would undoubtedly reflect this political sentiment.

Marlin T. Phelps, former justice of the Supreme Court of Arizona, spoke similarly of the Court.[8] In a broadcast on the Manion Forum entitled "Supreme Court — Communists' Most Precious Asset," Phelps attacked the Court for not adhering to the rules of strict Constitutional interpretation. "The majority of the members of the court," he said, "have resorted to every possible avenue of escape in order to reverse convictions of Communists affirmed by the circuit court of appeals . . ."[9] He accused the Court of viewing the Communist Party not as a conspiratorial organization, but as an "association entertaining beliefs or a beneficient ideology entirely innocent and harmless."[10]

Other judicial critics have been less bitter. Chief Justice John R. Dethmers of the Michigan Supreme Court, after professing a philosophy that the rights of the people are best safeguarded at the level of local government, stated that the current criticism of the Court was a good thing.[11] He urged citizens to become informed on the Court's actions so that they could criticize the opinions intelligently when necessary. Former Justice Dozier A. DeVane of the federal district court for Northern Florida, urged return to a more conservative judicial philosophy.[12] This can be effected, he said, only by a strict adherence to the doctrine of *stare decisis* and the rule of law.

In the more controversial decisions, one need go no further than the High Bench itself to find strong language. Justice McReynolds is reported to have remarked "this is Nero at his worst" with respect to the Gold Clause cases.[13] Justice Roberts in *Smith v. Allwright* noted that Supreme Court decisions appeared to be taking on the attributes of "restricted railroad tickets, valid only for the date of their issuance."[14] Justice Frankfurter, in the Tennessee apportionment case, stated that the majority opinion was a "massive repudiation of the experience of our whole past in asserting destructively novel judicial power."[15] Justice Jackson commented that "the rule of law is in unsafe hands when courts cease to function as courts and become organs for control of policy."[16] The justices themselves were advised to guard against a desire to exercise too much power. Former Chief Justice Harlan Fiske Stone noted that "while unconstitutional exercise of power by the executive and legislative branches of the government is subject to judicial restraint, the only check upon our own exercise of power is our own sense of self-restraint."[17]

Clearly the sanctity of the Court is not even recognized by its own members. Evidence of discontent among justices has been great and varied. Dissenting opinions have offered an excellent vehicle by which to manifest concern, and the justices have not hesitated to use them.

BAR CRITICS PUBLICIZED

While judges have contributed significantly to the criticism of the Supreme Court, their critiques have not received the public attention given to the attacks from the American Bar Association. Indeed, the relationship of the ABA to the political criticism of the Court is somewhat confused, possibly because there is not a consensus within the ABA on this issue. In addition, local bar associations have split with respect to their views on recent Supreme Court decisions.

During the earlier periods of contention, the various bar associations seemed to condone the actions of the Warren Court. The national association opposed the Jenner bill in 1958 (which was an attempt to limit the appellate jurisdiction of the Supreme Court), as did a wealth of local groups.[18] Perhaps the ABA was restrained by one of the canons of the association which states that "Judges, not being wholly free to defend themselves, are peculiarly entitled to receive the support of the Bar against unjust criticism and clamor."[19] Still, there appeared to be a great deal of disenchantment on the part of a large segment within the national organization with the substance of many of the controversial decisions. The canon pertained only to "unjust criticism." Hence the national bar apparently felt justified in its attack on the Court in 1959.

Even prior to the 1959 attack on the Court, there was a hint of things to come. At the 1957 annual convention, the ABA Committee on Communist Tactics, Strategy and Objectives called for legislation to overcome a number of recent Court decisions.[20] The House of Delegates, official body of the ABA, took no action on the recommendation, and the committee was simply advised to continue its study. Nevertheless, the report received a good deal of acclaim from the more articulate conservative critics. This created the impression that the ABA had taken issue with the Court's decisions, whereas in fact it had not. In order to combat the general impression of conservatism which the ABA was manifesting, one hundred lawyers, not representing the association, sent a resolution to Congress defending the Court from outside attacks.[21]

At the 1958 convention, the national organization took a stand opposing the passage of the Jenner bill,[22] but in so doing engaged in a heated battle on the score of some of its decisions. A delegate from Mississippi attempted to tack on to the anti-Jenner-bill resolution a statement to the effect that the Bar was disturbed with some of the Court's decisions as being contrary to recognized Constitutional precedent. Finally, as compromise, a clause was inserted stating that the Bar reserved the right to criticize decisions of the Court.

The 1959 annual convention produced the controversial resolutions which have been interpreted as a rebuke to the Court. Once again, the Committee on Communist Tactics, Strategy and Objectives submitted a lengthy report which literally ran the gamut of fears of the Communist threat. The committee gave its views on the Communist peace offensive, quoted from Fred Schwarz of the Christian Anti-Communist Crusade, questioned the wisdom of the present cultural exchange program, and condemned any attempts to recognize Red China or halt nuclear testing. In addition, it stated that "the paralysis of our internal security grows largely from construction and interpretation centering around technicalities emanating from our judicial process."[23] The committee went on to note that the Court had failed to recognize the "underground forces that are at work and to appreciate how these decisions affect our internal security."

The committee then proposed certain resolutions. Congress was urged to take appropriate steps to remedy the Court's decision in the *Watkins* case by clarifying the purpose of Congressional investigating committees, to rectify the *Nelson* case by expressing Congressional intention to disavow the doctrine of pre-emption, to prevent further decisions such as *Yates* by defining the concepts of "organize" and "advocacy" as found in the Smith Act, to require employees to swear allegiance to the United States, to permit summary dismissal of all governmental employees, to provide the executive with control over passports, and to strengthen the Foreign Agents Registration Act of 1948. These resolutions were adopted by the House of Delegates.[24]

Each of the recommendations fell within the purview of the legislature. Indeed, the Court itself had noted that it had ruled a particular way on several occasions because Congress had been silent with respect to its intention on certain issues. Taken by themselves, the ABA proposals do little more than demonstrate that the majority in the American Bar Association were concerned about the judicial results emanating from the Court. This is not out of tune with the conservatism which the ABA has always manifested.

A CONSERVATIVE HISTORY

Professor John Schmidhauser has pointed out that prior to 1937, the ABA had consistently supported the federal Supreme Court,[25] which at that time was predominantly conservative. The national bar opposed the Child-Labor bill, the National Health Insurance bill, the Ewing Health bill, and supported such proposals as the Tideland Oils bill and the Reed-Dirksen Amendment (placing a 25 per cent limit on income tax except under certain conditions).[26] When the Court did an about-face and began supporting the Roosevelt welfare legislation, Professor Schmidhauser noted that the ABA shifted loyalty to the more conservative state courts.

Response to the House of Delegates' adoption of the resolution of the Committee on Communist Tactics, Strategy and Objectives was immediate and heated. The American Civil Liberties Union, the Americans for Democratic Action, a number of local bar associations, and several noted legal academicians replied without delay.[27] ABA President Ross Malone felt it necessary to make a public statement of the fact that the House of Delegates had approved only the *recommendations* of the Committee on Communist Tactics, Strategy, and Objectives, and not the content of the report as a whole.[28] In spite of this statement, editorial writers, congressmen, and probably a large segment of the public appeared to interpret the ABA as endorsing the entire report. Senator Eastland, exploiting the full report for all it was worth, introduced approximately seven bills which he stated were proposed to carry out the recommendations of the ABA.[29]

In order to temper some of the damage to the Court's reputation arising from the report, the Philadelphia Bar Association felt the need to rebuke publicly the actions of the ABA.[30] And in a letter to the *New York Times*, Jefferson B. Fordham, Dean of the University of Pennsylvania Law School, also criticized the national bar association, not because it suggested statutory change, but rather because the report implied that the need for change arose from the Court not having done a good enough job.[31]

Taken out of context, the action of the House of Delegates on the committee's report was entirely proper. Undoubtedly, the majority of members of the ABA felt this action constituted "just" criticism within the purview of their canons of professional ethics. However, the timing of the endorsement all but nullified their good intentions. The recommendations were issued just as the general overall anti-Court feeling was beginning to ebb. There still remained, however, sufficient ill feeling for the ABA recommendations to rekindle the flames of controversy. Professor Phillip Kurland has pointed out that one of the main reasons for challenging the ABA committee pronouncements was that they gave aid and comfort to the "enemy."[32] This was especially true since the ABA holds the reputation, erroneous or not, of being a staunch defender of the judiciary. Thus its acceptance of the controversial report contributed an air of legitimacy not only to the well-intended critics of the Court, but also to those who had made reckless attacks.

It does appear that the ABA may have been somewhat less than judicious in its performance. A look at the membership of the Committee on Communist Tactics, Strategy and Objectives would have revealed that a strong anti-Court report would be forthcoming. The chairman of the committee was Peter C. Brown, unsuccessful counsel in the *Slochower* case, and former member of the Subversive Activities Control Board. Louis Wyman, the Attorney General in New Hampshire, whose investigation, prosecution, and conviction of Paul Sweezy were overturned by the Supreme Court only two years earlier, also served on the committee. Wyman had been one of the more vocal critics of the Court for several years. The character of the committee, plus realization that adverse criticism of the Court by the ABA would reinforce and legitimatize the claims of more radical critics, should have dictated more caution on behalf of the bar association in expressing its views on the Court's decisions.

ABA DISSENT CONTINUES

Dissent from the bar association did not cease with the 1959 dispute. As late as August 6, 1962, ABA President John C. Satterfield opened the eighty-fifth annual convention with a speech "denouncing" the Supreme Court. He made two principal charges: one that the Court was submerging state powers in a trend toward centralized government, and the other that "inordinate weight" was being given to individual rights in the areas of law enforcement and national security.[33] Several days later, a past president, Charles S. Rhyne, speaking to the American Law Student section of the national bar, defended the role of the Court and its decisions protecting individual rights.[34] He noted that Satterfield "was stating a personal opinion" and not the position of the ABA.

Many people have tended to posit a relationship between the ABA and the Court because of the Bar's campaign to bestow its stamp of approval on prospective Supreme Court appointees — a courtesy the ABA attempted for some time to obtain. Not until Eisenhower became President was this courtesy extended with any regularity. Then, having given approval to new appointees for an eight-year period, the Bar might be expected to defend these appointees against attack. It might be noted that President Kennedy did not extend the same courtesy to the Bar with respect to the appointments of Justice Byron White and Justice Arthur Goldberg. While ABA approval was extended, it was an after-the-fact gesture.

There is also a select group of professional critics whose criticism has been channeled through academic journals. For the most part these are law school professors and political scientists who have noted defects in some aspect of the judicial process. Little emphasis is placed by most of these critics on the political results of a judicial decision; rather, they are concerned with refining the methodological processes with which the justices work. Their concern is not so much with the "what" as with the "how" of decision-making.

A conspicuous exception to the above rule involves a group of liberal Court critics. For the most part, these have remained silent whenever the Court has offended them ideologically.

Apparently desirous of combating the attacks from the right, most liberal organizations have simply acquiesced to the Court's holdings. However, the volume of criticism from the right has reached such major proportions at times that several academicians have felt the need to demonstrate the fallacy of many of the conservative arguments. One way was to reveal that the Court's decisions were not necessarily cast in a liberal mold, but instead have actually been rather moderate. While pointing to this weakness in the conservative argument, a number of the liberal defenders also protested the Court's moderation in the area of civil liberties. Professor Harold Chase of the University of Minnesota has noted that the Warren Court has been too deferential and permissive to Congress to suit civil libertarians.[35] Arthur Keefe, professor of law at Catholic University of America, has taken a similar stand, arguing that the Court simply has not extended itself to protect individual liberty as it should.[36] Keefe would have the Court abandon a policy which he feels lacks clarity, certainty, and consistency in its opinions. According to Professor Keefe, a clear and definite stand must be taken by the Court in protecting the Bill of Rights and related questions under the Fourteenth Amendment.

ACADEMIC SUPPORT

Chase and Keefe have a number of liberal supporters in the academic world. Robert McCloskey of Harvard has reasoned that the Court is not "confronting the task of intellectual architecture that is posed by its modern jurisdictional claims in the field of civil rights."[37] His primary concern is that the justices failed to "develop a reasoned, connected set of doctrines in the field of civil rights." Fred Rodell of Yale, in his *Nine Men*, stresses the protection of individual liberties as of primary importance to the judicial function. Yet at the same time he notes that throughout the history of the Court, the justices have been "most bumblingly bashful, most reluctant to assert the autocratic power they hold . . . in the realm of civil liberties.[38]

Most of the liberal critics have this view of the Court's primary function as the promotion and protection of individual rights, and in this sense, they can be classified as part of the result-oriented school.

Yet this concern with results is fused with an academic perspective of the Court's role which is generally absent among the conservative result-oriented critics. Undoubtedly there are conservatives who relate the results of the Court's decisions to a states' rights philosophy. The unanswered question is whether these conservatives cherish the doctrine of states' rights for its own sake, or because for the present it serves the cause of conservatism. If the national government again were to become the champion of conservatism, and the states to assume the role of political activists, would the present advocates of states' rights continue to campaign for local control of political activity? This may prove to be a pertinent question if the Negro ever gains a voting edge in the South.

WECHSLER'S CRITICISM

Some of the most controversial criticism directed toward the Court of late was in an article written for the *Harvard Law Review*, by Professor Herbert Wechsler of Columbia Law School, entitled "Toward Neutral Principles in Constitutional Law."[39] Wechsler's article discusses a number of current academic issues ranging from judicial review to his main theme — the application of neutral principles in Constitutional adjudication.

Unlike the late Judge Learned Hand, Wechsler did not question the legitimacy of judicial review. The Columbia professor viewed the Supremacy Clause of the Constitution as giving judicial review a legitimate status, whereas Judge Hand found no formal grounds for judicial review, which he argues was simply conceived because the American political system had to have a final arbiter.[40] While Wechsler reasoned that judicial review must be regarded as an obligation, Hand insisted that it be used sparingly in order to prevent the Court from "transcending into the sphere of a third legislature."[41] Hand's formula for the exercise of judicial review is keyed to "how importunately the occasion demands an answer."[42] This latter narrow interpretation was used by many conservative critics to substantiate appeals for judicial self-restraint. Indeed, the judge's book on *The Bill of Rights* has been cited on numerous occasions to support conservative criticism of the Court. Hand's reference to the School Segregation cases classifies as a " coup de main,"[43] and his generally restrictive views of the judicial function go a long way to bolster the attacks.

Having dispensed with the general problem of judicial review, Wechsler appealed for the application of neutral principles in Constitutional adjudication. He noted that the "main constituent of the judicial process is precisely that it must be genuinely principled" and based upon "an analysis and reasons quite transcending the immediate result that is achieved."[44] In order to accomplish this, courts must decide cases upon grounds of "adequate neutrality and generality, tested not only by the instant application but by others that the principles imply."[45] In complying with this norm, courts will be unable to function as "naked power" organs because the adjudication will be predicated upon "principled decisions." Wechsler noted that this has been conspicuously absent in the ever-growing number of *per curiam* opinions handed down by the Court.

Wechsler's article on the application of neutral principles in constitutional adjudication found scholars lining up on both sides of the question. Louis Pollak of Yale tended to side "in principle" with Wechsler.[46] He did take issue, however, with the examples that Wechsler cites to substantiate this theory — the white primary, the restrictive covenant cases, and the School Segregation cases. In each instance, Pollak felt that the Court did incorporate a "rational and disinterested" application of Constitutional principles.

Louis Henkin of the University of Pennsylvania also accepted Wechsler's basic proposition, but like Pollak, felt the examples Wechsler chose were not illustrative of the problem.[47] Henkin argues that the Court "owes an obligation...to articulate the bases for its decisions — what ingredients have gone into the judgment, in what weights.."[48] A Court must be guided by "principled decisions" and it "must give reason that promises applicability to the next case."[49] At this point, Professor Henkin, like Wechsler, took the Court to task for rendering too many *per curiam* opinions.

The Wechsler-Pollak-Henkin appeal for the application of neutral principles in Constitutional adjudication gave rise to a school of Court defenders which regarded the call for neutral principles as not well-founded. Professors Addison Mueller and Murray Schwartz of UCLA, after noting the arguments of the neutral concepts school, took issue with the practicality of the Wechsler proposition.[50] In its simplest form, they argued, "neutrality means not taking sides." After analyzing the difficulties inherent in living up to such a doctrine, they concluded that the only cases which satisfy Professor Wechsler's theory are those involving the abdication of judicial review.

SIMILAR CONCLUSIONS

Professors Arthur S. Miller and Ronald S. Howell of Emory University came to a similar conclusion in an article entitled "The Myth of Neutrality in Constitutional Adjudication."[51] They asserted that adherence to neutral principles in Constitutional adjudication is simply impossible. In attempting to substantiate their theory, they drew support from such men as Plato, Karl Mannheim, Gunnar Myrdal, Isaiah Berlin and Reinhold Neibuhr, all of whom believed that a neutral process is not attainable in either the social or natural sciences. The Emory University professors reasoned that throughout American Constitutional development, justices have been motivated by value preferences and not concepts of neutrality, in reaching decisions. Miller and Howell suggest that judicial decisions should be "gauged by their results and not by their coincidence with a set of allegedly consistent doctrinal principles or by an impossible reference to neutrality of principle." [52]

A third member of the anti-Wechsler school is Benjamin Wright of the University of Texas. In a paper delivered before the 1961 annual meeting to the American Political Science Association, Professor Wright attempted to analyze the Wechsler position.[53] According to Wright, Wechsler never defines what he means by "neutral." After questioning whether the Columbia professor does not really mean "well established and generally accepted" principles, Wright noted that neutrality is a non-existent concept. Wright further took issue with Wechsler's view of Chief Justice Marshall and Justice Holmes as being neutral in their application of Constitutional principles. Wright looked upon their actions as predominantly partisan. Witness Marshall's decision in *Marbury v. Madison* and Holmes' approach to the fundamental freedom cases. Finally, Wright felt that Wechsler offered no guide for facing new Constitutional issues, or for bringing the meaning of the Constitution into harmony with the political realities of the times.[54]

TWO SCHOOLS OF THOUGHT

Differences of opinion over the application of neutral principles in Constitutional adjudication will probably provide vigorous academic exercise for many years to come, because of the schism of belief between two schools of thought — the result-oriented and process-oriented — with respect to the manner in which the Supreme Court approaches its cases. Though attention is focused to a degree upon the results of judicial decision, this is not done from a partisan point of view; rather, results are stressed because the result of a number of decisions is often inextricably entwined with the process of decision-making.

An instance in which academic criticism of the Supreme Court was very much in the public eye occurred during the 1957-58 anti-Court campaign. It involved the late Edward S. Corwin, a noted authority on Constitutional Law. The former professor emeritus from Princeton University felt compelled to enunciate his views on recent Supreme Court decisions involving Communists. Following the Court's four decisions handed down on "Red Monday,"[55] Corwin wrote a letter to the *New York Times* in which he stated that the Court's theorizing in the *Yates* case was "nonsensical, and represents...a recent tenderizing of the judicial mind toward the American Communist Party."[56] Professor Corwin's views manifesting a preference for national security are well pointed out in his book *The Constitution and What It Means Today*.[57] When asked to testify in favor of the Jenner bill in 1958, Corwin had to refuse because of illness, but statements from his book were inserted into the record.

The Princeton professor did, however, take pen in hand to convey his ideas in a letter to the *New York Times*.[58] He alluded to the fact that the Jenner bill coped with a very urgent problem, i.e., keeping the Court out of legislative territory, and, he cites Judge Learned Hand as agreeing with him. Corwin also found a number of things wrong with the Jenner bill, but then continued to state: "There can be no doubt that on June 17 last, the Court went on a virtual binge and thrust its nose into matters beyond its competence with the result that in my judgment, it should have its aforesaid nose well tweaked."[59] He viewed the holding in the *Watkins* decision as "irresponsible and indefensible." *Yates* was equally irresponsible and the *Cole* case was "weird." Finally, Corwin called for legislation "assertive of the correct reading of the Constitution and the points involved in [these] cases."

CRAFTSMANSHIP CRITICIZED

The art of legal "craftsmanship" has also served as a focal point for a number of the Court's academic critics. Among others, Professor Henry M. Hart, Jr., of Harvard Law School, has evidenced a good deal of concern over the problems of craftsmanship and judicial administration.[60] Hart believes that the Court is attempting to decide more cases than it can decide well. As a result, he finds that too few of the Court's opinions "genuinely illumine the area of the law with which they deal,"[61] and issues are ignored which in good lawyership and good conscience ought not to be. These failures supposedly are undermining the respect of what Hart termed "first rate lawyers" for the incumbent justices. Professor Hart feels that it is not merely the shortness of time that has hindered the Court. Equally important is the paucity of "collective deliberation" on behalf of the justices. He feels that the justices have a tendency to arrive at a decision even prior to deliberation. The solution to the problem requires that opinions be "grounded in reason and not mere fiat or precedent." In this argument, Hart's criticism is not unlike that of the Wechsler school.

His argument that the burden of work is much too great and results in a lack of good lawyership was greeted by other authorities with mixed emotions. Judge Thurman Arnold immediately characterized Hart's article as a series of "pompous generalizations."[62] Arnold appeared to view Hart's criticism as that of a partisan distressed with the liberal trend of decisions. With respect to Hart's appeal for "durable principles" of law, Arnold noted that many of these so-called "durable principles" have been forced "to yield to new times and new experiences."[63] He pointed out that conferences of collective thought by the justices as advocated by Professor Hart would not necessarily bring forth a victory of reason over the present juridical philosophies. In all probability they would do no more than reinforce the justices' respective ideals. In closing, Judge Arnold defined the "first rate lawyers" to which Hart refers as members of the ABA and large corporation lawyers who have at times been the Court's most adamant critics with respect to liberal opinions.

REACTIONS MORE FAVORABLE

Other reactions to Hart's criticism were much more favorable. Dean Erwin Griswold also emphasized a need to lighten the Court's load of work.[64] He noted that while Judge Arnold was stating that the Court was not overworked, Justice Stewart, while addressing the annual dinner of the *Yale Law Journal*, said that the "case load of the Court is demonstratively a heavy one."[65] Dean Griswold thought that it was incumbent upon the American Bar Association to take the lead in developing legislation which would reduce the burden. Professor Paul Freund of Harvard was another Hart supporter in the belief that the Court is overworked. Freund suggested that the situation could be eradicated if the Court would adopt "stricter, more Brandeisian standards in the granting of review."[66]

In addition to the problem of the work load, Freund echoed Professor Hart's criticism of the craftsmanship of the Court. He reasoned that there is a tendency to "make broad principles do service for specific problems that call for differentiation, a tendency toward overbroadness that is not an augury of enduring work...."[67] In such instances, the Court, according to Freund, "misses the opportunity to use the litigation process for the refinement and adoption of principle to meet the variety of concrete issues as they are presented in a lawsuit."[68] Professor McClosky, as noted earlier, related this broad problem to the issue of civil rights. He asked why the Court has done so little to develop a reasoned, connected set of doctrines in the field of civil rights."[69] McClosky noted that the "Court is not confronting the task of intellectual architecture that is posed by its modern jurisdictional claims..."

Another problem upsetting professional critics concerns the rendering of an excessive number of *per curiam* opinions. Professor Ernest Brown of Harvard Law School has expressed his concern with the increased number of "summary procedures."[70] Brown feels that this type of activity smacks of "predetermined purpose." Much of this, according to Brown, is attributable to the quantitative burden the Court must assume. Wechsler and Henkin also hold this view.

TOO MANY GENERALIZATIONS

From Yale, Alexander Bickel and Harry Wellington have fused the problem of *per curiam* opinions with the Court's tendency to overgeneralize they note that "The Court's product has shown an increasing incidence of the sweeping dogmatic statement, of the formulation of results accompanied by little or no effort to support them in reason...."[71] This, coupled with an increasing number of *per curiam* orders, has failed to "build the bridge between the authorities they cite and the results they decree."[72] The Yale professors express concern over the fact that the Court apparently no longer feels the need to "explain its conclusions, to justify them and to relate them to its past holdings."[73]

This brief sketch of judicial criticism reveals a number of problems which have distressed the academic critics: failure to adopt neutral principles in Constitutional adjudication, inadequate legal craftsmanship, excessive rendering of *per curiam* opinions, insufficient reasoning to support decisions, pre-conceived ideas with respect to a decision—all sensitive issues. Feelings in this area are strong and deep because the criticism expounded is always fused with a jurisprudential base. Unlike the attacks emanating from Congress and the non-governmental critics, a large portion of the professional critics have divorced their suggestions and criticism from emotional and irrational overtones. There have, it is true, been instances in which the critiques of the professionals manifested an especially bitter dissent. Noteworthy among these were the attacks reported from former Supreme Court Justice James Byrnes and Professor Edward S. Corwin. These, however, proved to be exceptions to the general rule.

8. LEARNING TO LIVE WITH THE CRITICS

Viewed as a whole, the attacks on the Warren Court foreshadow the critical atmosphere in which the judiciary must function for years to come. The barrage of criticism in recent years has undoubtedly gone a long way to destroy the myth that the Supreme Court is immune to political scrutiny. Yet vulnerable as the Court is, it surely will have to continue to deal with a host of controversial social and political issues affecting the public at large. Thus, critical response from the groups adversely affected seems inevitable.

It is difficult to say whether criticism of the Court will result again in such intense feeling as characterized the abortive attempt in 1957-58 to limit the power of the judiciary. To a large extent this will depend on the issues involved. The earlier controversy was provoked by conservative fear of what was regarded as the Court's overly sympathetic attitude toward individual rights as against protection from the internal threat of Communism. Whether this issue will be revived or will be replaced by a new social problem is hard to predict.

However, it is possible to point to some factors which may help to perpetuate anti-Court criticism. First of these is the explosive disagreement following the Court decision on legislative apportionment. [1]

In establishing "one man, one vote," as the criterion for apportioning, not only the House of Representatives, but both houses of the state legislatures as well, the justices opened a Pandora's box of political discontent. It may be expected that as urban forces gain strength by agitating for more "rational" apportionment schemes, the rural power-elite will increase its attacks upon the "one-man, one vote" philosophy. This could provide impetus to an anti-Court campaign reaching well into the future. In the mid-Sixties twenty-one states had already passed resolutions calling for a Constitutional amendment, either to prevent the Court from assuming jurisdiction over apportionment cases, or by some other means to negate the effect of "one-man, one vote."

The question of religion in the public schools provides another sensitive area likely to breed controversy. The Court's holding in the School Prayer case[2] dealt only with a narrow issue — the question of whether a state may compose a non-denominational prayer to be read at the opening of each public school session. This is but one of the religion-in-public-school issues which eventually will come before the Court. Currently underway is a movement for a Constitutional amendment legalizing prayer and Bible-reading in the public schools. The Court will undoubtedly become the subject of additional attack as this amendment is brought to public attention.

In addition to the provocative effect of substantive issues, there is the change in the Court's personnel. Justice Whittaker and Justice Frankfurter have both retired. Whittaker was replaced by former Deputy Attorney General Byron B. White, and the late President Kennedy appointed Secretary of Labor Arthur J. Goldberg to the seat held by Frankfurter. In 1965, Justice Goldberg left the Court to assume the United Nations vacancy created by the death of Adlai Stevenson. Goldberg was replaced by Abe Fortas, a liberal attorney from Washington, D.C.

It is hazardous to predict how an individual elevated to the Supreme Court will vote. Justice White is generally considered to have moved in the direction of the conservative members. Goldberg, on the other hand, firmly established himself as a member of the liberal bloc previously made up of Warren, Black, Douglas, and Brennan. It is assumed that Fortas will follow in Goldberg's footsteps. This point becomes especially interesting in view of the fact that many of the Court's conservative decisions in the past have been decided on a 5-4 voting basis. Both Whittaker and Frankfurter sided with the so-called conservative coalition on frequent occasions, including three key 5-4 decisions (*Barenblatt v. United States, Uphaus v. Wyman,* and *Nelson and Globe v. Los Angeles*), each of which supposedly modified earlier liberal decisions upholding the rights of individuals (the *Watkins, Sweezy,* and *Slochower* cases discussed in Chapter 3). If Justice Fortas does side with the liberals in public offender cases, thereby perpetuating the bloc's majority position, the 1957-58 controversy could be revived.

COMMON UNDERSTANDING NEEDED

This review of Court criticism has showed it arising from several different sources, with Congress as perhaps the most frequent and vocal point of origin. This frequency notwithstanding, a recent study of congressional attempts to reverse Court decisions has indicated that they are seldom successful in the absence of a "common understanding" among the legislators disrupted by a particular decision.[3] In nearly every instance where Congress has been effective, there has been "almost unanimous support of the politically articulate groups affected by the Court's decision."[4] Decisions which generated mixed reactions have been seldom if ever overruled.

The current congressional attitude toward decisions reveals very little consensus. It has been shown that the bulk of judicial attacks has emanated from a loose-knit coalition of Southern Democrats and conservative Republicans. Although a multitude of bills has been proposed to remedy the judicial-legislative dispute, most of them have come from Congressmen with relatively little influence. Whenever more powerful legislators have entered the fray, they have done so more in terms of rhetoric than of political action. Of all the bills submitted, only one — the Jencks Act — has become a law. The other determined congressional effort to chastise the Court was the abortive proposal known as the Jenner bill, an omnibus which sought and failed to limit the Court's appellate jurisdiction.

As the conflicts of opinion endure — lying dormant at times — and then are revitalized by hotly contested decisions, Congress will doubtless continue to serve as a chief forum for judicial criticism. This can be beneficial if the legislators will bear in mind the thoughts of former Senator Kenneth Keating:

> The proper way to respond . . . is not by attacks on the membership or authority of the Court. The proper response is by studying in mature and measured manner the problems raised by any decision of the Court, and then if necessary, by proposing legislation to offset any serious defects which might arise out of these decisions.[5]

All too often in the recent past congressional critics of the Court — in particular the conservative critics — have not managed to meet such standards. In particular, the Radical Right has used the floor of Congress to attempt suppression of the powers of the judiciary. Such attempts have been characterized by irrationality and emotion, and — except in the case of the John Birch Society and the Christian Crusade — a lack of cohesion and effective organization.

STATE ATTACKS SIMILAR

State-nurtured attacks on the Court have followed a pattern similar to that of congressional attack, with the additional motivation of the states' resentment over a continuing increase in federal power. Here as in other sources of attack, the question of segregation has been a significant factor in the attempt of some states to interpose their sovereignty against the Court's degrees. Attacks have come also from law enforcement agents, arguing the inhibiting effect of Court decisions on police functions. In this connection the FBI succeeded in bringing about enactment of the Jencks bill — the only anti-Court measure ever actually passed by Congress. Consequent upon this particular group of objections have been recent attempts on the part of officials to sophisticate their training techniques in order to comply with the new guidelines for law enforcement. Also, these officials, along with other experts in the fields of Constitutional and criminal law, are drafting model codes for present and future police practices.

PROFESSIONALS CONSTRUCTIVE

Most constructive of all criticism of the judiciary, however, has undoubtedly been that of the professional critics — especially those academicians who thoughtfully and purposefully have pointed to weaknesses in the judicial process. Reasoned analysis rather than irrational harangue has been the temper of this criticism, which has come to play a meaningful role in the refinement and strengthening of the entire judicial system.

In any event, criticism of the Supreme Court and its decisions has now acquired a rich and active history and can probably look forward to an equally vigorous future. For every decision that the High Bench hands down, there are bound to be groups overjoyed and other groups left "hurting." Both of these kinds of reactions appear to be a necessary — perhaps even a healthy — attribute of the process of adjudication in a diverse and dynamic modern society.

NOTES

NOTES TO CHAPTER 1

1. Keith Wheeler, "Who's Who in the Tumult of the Far Right," *Life* (Feb. 9, 1962), 110, 118.

2. David J. Brewer, "Government by Injunction," *Nat'l Corp. Rep.*, XV (1898), 848, 849.

3. Erwin N. Griswold, "Foreword: Of Time and Attitudes — Professor Hart and Judge Arnold." 74 *Harv. L. Rev.* 81 (1960).

4. C. Herman Pritchett, *Congress Versus the Supreme Court* (Minne., 1961).

5. Walter F. Murphy, *Congress and the Court* (Chicago, 1962).

6. *Ibid.*, vii.

7. The Presidency is excluded as a source since it has been conspicuously absent from among the Court's critics during the past decade.

8. *Watkins v. United States,* 354 *U.S.* 178 (1957).

9. *Mallory v. United States*. 354 *U.S.* 449 (1957).

10. This is the term used by Anthony Lewis to describe one of the molds of criticism in "The Supreme Court and Its Critics," 48 *Minne. L. Rev.* 305 (1961).

11. Joseph F. Menez, "A Brief in Support of the Supreme Court," 54 *Northwestern L. Rev.* 30, 31 (1959-60).

12. Bernard Schwartz, "Is Criticism of the High Court Valid?" *New York Times Magazine* (August 26, 1957), 14.

13. Phillip Kurland, "The Supreme Court and Its Judicial Critics," 6 *Utah L. Rev.* 457 (1959).

14. Charles Horsky, "Law Day: Some Reflections on The Current Proposals to Curb The Supreme Court," 42 *Minne. L. Rev.* 1105, 1108 (1958).

15. 103 *Congressional Record*, 85th Cong., 1st Sess. (1957), 10,672.

16. *Watkins v. United States,* 354 *U.S.* 178 (1957). In a contempt of Congress case, the Court reversed Watkins' conviction on the ground that the House Un-American Activities Committee had not apprised the witness why the questions propounded to him were pertinent to the investigation.
Yates v. United States, 354 *U.S.* 298 (1957). Here the Court narrowly defined the "organizational" and "advocacy" clauses of the Smith Act resulting in the reversal

of five lower federal court convictions.

Sweezy v. New Hampshire, 354 *U.S.* 234 (1957). In this case the Court held that New Hampshire had not provided an adequate basis for controlling the State Attorney General's one-man investigation into subversive activities.

Service v. Dulles, 354 *U.S.* 363 (1957). In this case, the Court held that the Secretary of State had not complied with the State Department's regulation in discharging the petitioner who had been classified a security risk by the Loyalty Review Board.

17. *Barenblatt v. United States,* 360 *U.S.* 109 (1959).

18. *Uphaus v. Wyman,* 360 *U.S.* 72 (1959).

19. 350 *U.S.* 551 (1956).

20. *Nelson and Globe v. Los Angeles,* 362 *U.S.* 1 (1960); also see *Beilan v. Board of Education,* 357 *U.S.* 399 (1958), and *Lerner v. Casey,* 357 *U.S.* 468 (1958).

21. *Braden v. United States,* 365 *U.S.* 431 (1961); *Wilkinson v. United States,* 365 *U.S.* 399 (1961).

22. *Abel v. United States,* 362 *U.S.* 217 (1960); *Scales v. United States,* 367 *U.S.* 203 (1961).

23. *Baker v. Carr,* 369 *U.S.* 186 (1962); *Colegrove v. Green,* 328 *U.S.* 549 (1946).
    The *Colegrove* case held that the problem of apportionment was a political question, and hence, did not fall within the Supreme Court's jurisdiction (a non-justiciable issue).

24. *New York Times* (Mar. 28, 1962), 1.

25. *Idem.*

26. 108 *Congressional Record,* 87th Cong., 2nd Sess. (1962), 7026 *et seq.*

NOTES TO CHAPTER 2

1. 347 *U.S.* 483 (1954).

2. These bills were compiled through an examination of the *Digest of General and Public Bills* between 1954-1961. Undoubtedly a number of bills were overlooked because many were hidden in provisions of general bills unrelated to the instant area of concern.

3. The states included: Alabama, Arkansas, Florida, Georgia, Louisiana, Mississippi, North Carolina, South Carolina, Tennessee, Texas, and Virginia.

4. 102 *Congressional Record,* 84th Cong., 2nd Sess. (1956), 4460, 4515.

5. *Idem.*

6. Alexander M. Bickel, "Ninety Six Congressmen Versus the Nine Justices," *New Republic* (April 23, 1956), 11.

7. 103 *Congressional Record,* 85th Cong., 1st Sess. (1957), 4012.

8. 352 *U.S.* 191 (1957). Fikes was a Negro of limited intelligence who had been sentenced to death for commiting burglary with attempt to rape. His conviction was reversed by the Supreme Court because he had been held incommunicado for a week and questioned intermittently before arraignment.

9. 103 *Congressional Record,* 85th Cong., 1st Sess. (1957), 4012.

10. *Ibid.,* 4340.

11. *Ibid.,* 15714.

12. H. J. Res. 14, 87/1 (1961), H. J. Res. 260, 86/1 (1959), H. J. Res. 18, 87/1 (1961), H. J. Res. 295, 86/1 (1959), H. J. Res. 133, 87/1 (1961), H. J. Res. 258, 86/1 (1959), H. J. Res. 299, 87/1 (1961).

13. S. J. Res. 30, 87/1 (1961). Co-sponsors of this bill included Senators Byrd (D. Va.), Johnston (D. S.Carol.), Hill (D. Ala.), Eastland (D. Miss.), Sparkman (D. Ala.), Stennis (D. Miss.), Long (D. Ga.), and Robertson (D. Va.).

14. 163 *U.S.* 537 (1896).

15. S. J. Res. 137, 84/2 (1956).

16. H. J. Res. 568, 84/2 (1956), H. J. Res. 570, 84/2 (1956), H. J. Res. 571, 84/2 (1956).

17. H. J. Res. 532, 83/2 (1954).

18. S. 3467, 85/2 (1958), S. 1016, 84/1 (1955), H. R. 1228, 85/1 (1957), H. R. 175, 85/1 (1957), H. R. 3769, 84/1 (1955).

19. S. 412, 87/1 (1961), H. R. 1192, 87/1 (1961), H.R. 2933, 87/1 (1961).

20. S. J. Res. 159, 83/2 (1954), S. J. Res. 75, 85/1 (1957), H. J. Res. 102, 86/1 (1959), H. J. Res. 394, 85/1 (1957), H. J. Res. 458, 85/1 (1957), H. J. Res. 559, 84/2 (1956), H. J. Res. 282, 84/1 (1955).

21. H. J. Res. 495, 84/2 (1956).

22. H. J. Res. 587, 87/1 (1961).

23. 103 *Congressional Record,* 85th Cong. 1st Sess. (1957), 10333.

24. 103 *Congressional Record,* 85th Cong. 1st Sess. (1957), A5150.

25. 104 *Congressional Record,* 85th Cong. 2nd Sess. (1958), 12121.

26. 108 *Congressional Record,* 87th Cong. 2nd Sess. (1962), 7026 *et seq.*

27. *Idem.*

28. James O. Eastland, "The Supreme Court — A Revolutionary Tribunal," *Manion Forum Network,* Weekly Broadcast No. 252 (South Bend, July 26, 1959).

29. *Idem.*

30. 105 *Congressional Record,* 86th Cong., 1st Sess. (1959), 7505.

31. 102 *Congressional Record,* 84th Cong., 2nd Sess. (1956), 6386.

32. 106 *Congressional Record,* 86th Cong., 2nd Sess. (1960), 3530.

33. *Idem.*

34. William E. Jenner, "The Supreme Court," *American Mercury,* LXXXVI (March, 1958), 27.

35. 103 *Congressional Record,* 85th Cong., 1st Sess. (1957), 10534.

36. *Ibid.,* 10526.

37. *Ibid.,* 10525.

38. 103 *Congressional Record,* 85th Cong., 1st Sess. (1957), 10542.

39. 104 *Congressional Record,* 85th Cong., 2nd Sess. (1958), 2011.

40. 103 *Congressional Record,* 85th Cong., 1st Sess. (1957), 10188.

41. H. R. 7914, 87/1 (1961).

42. S. 409, 87/1 (1961). Also see S. 1184, 85/1 (1957).

43. See John Schmidhauser, *The Supreme Court: Its Politics, Personalities and Procedures* (1960), p. 83 *et seq.*

44. H. R. 12143, 84/2 (1956).

45. S. 3811, 84/2 (1956), and H. R. 9215, 83/2 (1954).

46. H. R. 4393, 87/1 (1961).

47. H. R. 1200, 86/1 (1959), H. R. 7753, 87/1 (1961), S. 1440, 84/1 (1955), and S. 264, 84/2 (1956).

48. H. R. 534, 87/1· (1961), H. R. 320, 86/1 (1959), H. R. 2270, 86/1 (1959), H. R. 11374, 84/2 (1956).

49. H. J. Res. 407, 85/1 (1957), H. J. Res. 415, 85/1 (1957), H. J. Res. 136, 86/1 (1959), H. J. Res. 388, 85/1 (1957).

50. S. J. Res. 114, 85/1 (1957), H. J. Res. 403, 85/1 (1957).

51. S. J. Res. 114, 85/1 (1957).

52. S. J. Res. 168, 84/2 (1956).
53. S. J. Res. 7, 86/1 (1959).
54. H. J. Res. 141, 87/1 (1961).
55. 103 *Congressional Record,* 85th Cong., 1st Sess. (1957), 10187.
56. H. J. Res. 406, 85/1 (1957).
57. See John Schmidhauser's discussion of this problem in *The Supreme Court: Its Politics, Personalities and Procedures* (N.Y., 1960).
58. H. J. Res. 428, 85/1 (1957).
59. H. J. Res. 536, 85/2 (1958).
60. 103 *Congressional Record,* 85th Cong., 1st Sess. (1957), 9889.
61. H. J. Res. 395, 85/1 (1957).
62. H. R. 4565, 86/1 (1959), and H. R. 4659, 86/1 (1959).
63. H. R. 5750, 87/1 (1961).
64. H. R. 404, 87/1 (1961).
65. H. R. 11795, 84/2 (1956).
66. H. J. Res. 201, 84/1 (1959). Also see H. R. 70, 87/1 (1961).
67. H. J. Res. 134, 86/1 (1959). Also see H. J. Res. 103, 86/1 (1959).
68. 103 *Congressional Record,* 85th Cong., 1st Sess. (1957), 10188.
69. This will be discussed in more detail in Chapter VI.
70. 103 *Congressional Record,* 85th Cong., 1st Sess. (1957), 16160.
71. This is a study of the economic, sociological, and psychological problems the Negro must face under the American democratic system of government.
72. 103 *Congressional Record,* 85th Cong., 1st Sess. (1957), A4218.
73. 106 *Congressional Record,* 86th Cong., 2nd Sess. (1960), 3530.
74. William H. Rehnquist, "Who Writes the Decisions of the Supreme Court," *U.S. News and World Report,* XXXXIII (Dec. 13, 1957), 75.
75. *Idem.*
76. John Stennis, "Investigate Supreme Court's 'law clerk' System," *Ibid.,* XXXXIV (May 16, 1958), 117.
77. 103 *Congressional Record,* 85th Cong., 1st Sess. (1957), 572.
78. 105 *Congressional Record,* 86th Cong., 1st Sess. (1959), 16302.
79. 103 *Congressional Record,* 85th Cong., 1st Sess. (1957), 11817.
80. *Ibid.,* 16979.
81. 103 *Congressional Record,* 85th Cong., 1st Sess. (1957), 10123.
82. *Idem.*
83. *Philadelphia Inquirer* (June 25, 1957), as quoted in Murphy, p. 117.
84. S. 2646, 85/2 (1958). Details of these decisions are presented in Chapter III.
85. 103 *Congressional Record,* 85th Cong., 1st Sess. (1957), 12809.
86. *Ibid.,* 12806-10.
87. *Ibid.,* A4928.
88. Here the Court upheld the contempt of Congress conviction of a college professor thereby acquiescing to the Congressional authorizing resolution to the House Un-American Activities Committee.
89. H. R. 756, 87/1 (1961).
90. *Washington Post* (Feb. 27, 1958), 6-B.
91. 105 *Congressional Record,* 86th Cong., 1st Sess. (1959), 7505.

92. 103 *Congressional Record,* 85th Cong., 1st Sess. (1957), 10525.

93. 105 *Congressional Record,* 86th Cong., 1st Sess. (1959), 3023.

94. U.S. Congress, Senate, Internal Security Subcommittee, *Hearings on S. 2646,* 85th Cong., 2nd Sess. (1958), p. 208.

95. *Ibid.,* p. 297.

96. Joseph Menez, "A Brief in Support of the Supreme Court," 54 *Northwestern L. Rev.* 30 (1959).

97. Paul Freund, "The Supreme Court Crisis," an address at Brandeis University (Nov. 12, 1958); Harold W. Chase, "The Warren Court and Congress," 44 *Minne. L. Rev.* 595 (1960).

98. 106 *Congressional Record,* 86th Cong., 2nd Sess. (1960), 5232.

NOTES TO CHAPTER 3

1. Since considerable attention was devoted to the School Segregation cases in Chapter II, further elaboration here would only be repetitious.

2. 354 *U.S.* 298 (1957).

3. 18 *U.S.C.A.* 2385 (1940).

4. 225 *F.2nd* 146 (1955).

5. S. 2646, 85/2 (1958). Reported, but passed over.

6. S. 527, 86/1 (1959).

7. H. R. 6, 87/1 (1961). Also see: H. R. 3247, 87/1 (1961) — passed House; S. 2653, 86/2 (1960) — reported, but passed over; S. 1305, 86/1 (1959); and H. R. 2369, 86/1 (1959) — passed House.

8. H. R. 2369, 86/1 (1959).

9. 354 *U.S.* 234 (1957).

10. S. 2646, 85/2 (1958). The Jenner bill was reported out of committee, but never passed the Senate. No other bills dealing with the *Sweezy* case reached the floor of either house.

11. 354 *U.S.* 178 (1957).

12. See Carl Beck, *Contempt of Congress* (New Orleans, 1959), p. 158 *et seq.* for a detailed analysis of the Warren opinion.

13. 354 *U.S.* 178,202 (1957).

14. *Ibid.,* 200.

15. *Ibid.,* 187.

16. S. 2646, 85/2 (1958). Also see: H. R. 10775, 86/2 (1958), H. R. 654, 87/1 (1961), and H. R. 756, 87/1 (1961). Only S. 2646 was reported out of committee.

17. 354 *U.S.* 363 (1957).

18. *Ibid.,* 369.

19. 349 *U.S.* 331 (1955).

20. 351 *U.S.* 536 (1956).

21. S. 2646, 85/2 (1958).

22. See Murphy and Pritchett, *Courts, Judges, and Politics* (New York, 1961), p. 174, for a discussion of this movement.

23. S. 1411, 85/2 (1958).

24. 104 *Congressional Record,* 85th Cong., 1st Sess. (1957), 13401-17.

25. H. R. 1870, 86/1 (1959).

26. S. 1304, 86/1 (1959).

27. H. R. 6, 87/1 (1961). Also see H. R. 756, 87/1 (1961).

28. 360 *U.S.* 474 (1959).

29. *Ibid.*, 508.

30. H. R. 8121, 86/1 (1959).

31. S. 2314, 2392, 2416, 86/1 (1959).

32. C. Herman Pritchett, *Congress Versus the Supreme Court* (Minneapolis, 1961), p. 106.

33. 357 *U.S.* 116 (1958).

34. *Ibid.*, 121. The Internal Security Act of 1950 forbidding passports to members of Communist organizations required to register with the Attorney General was not effective at this time; hence, no organizations had registered under the law.

35. 104 *Congressional Record*, 85th Cong., 2nd Sess. (1958), 14089.

36. *Ibid.*, 13406.

37. S. 4110, 85/2 (1958).

38. H. R. 9069, 86/1 (1959).

39. See Pritchett, pp. 90-91 for a discussion of the details of H. R. 9069, (1959).

40. 353 *U.S.* 657 (1957).

41. *Ibid.*, 681-82.

42. 103 *Congressional Record*, 85th Cong., 1st Sess. (1957), 10741.

43. *Ibid.*, 10614.

44. 103 *Congressional Record*, 85th Cong., 2nd Sess. (1958), 16981.

45. S. 2377, 85/1 (1957).

46. See Walter Murphy, *Congress and the Court* (Chicago, 1962), pp. 130-153, for an excellent discussion of the political ramifications involving the passage of the Jencks bill.

47. 350 *U.S.* 497 (1956).

48. The scheme of federal regulation included the Smith Act, the Internal Security Act of 1950, and the Communist Control Act of 1954.

49. 350 *U.S.* 497, 500 (1956).

50. 102 *Congressional Record*, 84th Cong., 2nd Sess. (1956), 6383.

51. *Ibid.*, 6384.

52. *Idem.*

53. *Idem.*

54. *Ibid.*, 6386.

55. H. R. 3, 85/1 (1957).

56. S. 337 and S. 654, 85/1 (1957).

57. Pritchett, p. 78.

58. See Murphy, p. 193 *et seq.*

59. 105 *Congressional Record*, 85th Cong., 2nd Sess. (1958), 11803.

60. *Ibid.*, 11498.

61. *Ibid.*, 11641.

62. 353 *U.S.* 232 (1957).

63. 353 *U.S.* 252 (1957).

64. No convictions resulted from any of Schware's arrests.

65. 350 *U.S.* 551 (1956).

66. 102 *Congressional Record*, 84th Cong., 2nd Sess. (1956), 6384.

67. 103 *Congressional Record*, 85th Cong., 1st Sess. (1957), 6834.

68. 104 *Congressional Record*, 85th Cong., 2nd Sess. (1958), 18687.

69. See *Lerner v. Casey*, 357 *U.S.* 468 (1958), *Beilan v. Board of Education*, 357 *U.S.* 399 (1958), and *Nelson and Globe v. County of Los Angeles*, 362 *U.S.* 1 (1960).

70. 354 *U.S.* 449 (1957).

71. 318 *U.S.* 322 (1943). In this case, two suspects were questioned over a period of two days before arraignment. The confession, which was obtained during the two day period, was held to be inadmissible as evidence.

72. 18 *U.S.C.A.* 5 (a) (1952).

73. 103 *Congressional Record,* 85th Cong., 1st Sess. (1957), 10471.

74. See S. 525, 86/1 (1959), H. R. 8624, 85/1 (1957), H. R. 8600, 85/1 (1957), H. R. 8596, 85/1 (1957).

75. H. R. 4957, 85/2 (1958).

76. Alan Barth, *The Price of Liberty* (New York, 1961), XI.

77. *Colegrove v. Green,* 328 *U.S.* 549 (1946).

78. 369 *U.S.* 186 (1962).

79. 372 *U.S.* 368 (1963).

80. *Ibid.,* 381.

81. 376 *U.S.* 1 (1964).

82. 84 *S. Ct.* 1362 (1964). See also: *W.M.C.A. v. Lomenzo,* 84 *S. Ct.* 1418 (1964), *Maryland Committee for Fair Representation v. Tawes,* 84 *S. Ct.* 1442 (1964), *Davis v. Mann,* 84 *S. Ct.* 1453 (1964), *Roman v. Sincock,* 84 *S. Ct.* 1462 (1964), and *Lucas v. Forty-Fourth General Assembly of Colorado,* 84 *S. Ct.* 1472 (1964). There are some important differences in these cases, but they need not be analyzed for purposes of the instant study.

83. See *Congressional Quarterly Guide to Current American Government* (Fall, 1964), p. 53 *et seq.* for background on this issue.

84. H. R. 11926, 88/2 (1964).

85. *Congressional Quarterly Guide to Current American Government* (Spring, 1965), p. 44.

86. S. 3069, 88/2 (1964).

87. *Congressional Quarterly Guide to Current American Government* (Spring, 1965), p. 44.

88. *Engel v. Vitale,* 370 *U.S.* 421 (1962).

89. 108 *Congressional Record,* 87th Cong., 2nd Sess (1962), 11719.

90. *Ibid.,* 11675.

91. *Ibid.,* 11732.

92. *Ibid.,* 11718.

93. *Ibid.,* 11719.

94. *New York Times* (July 1, 1962), E-9.

95. 108 *Congressional Record,* 87th Cong., 2nd Sess. (1962), 10884.

96. *Pittsburgh Press* (June 26, 1962), 1.

97. 108 *Congressional Record,* 87th Cong., 2nd Sess. (1962), 11719, 11669, 12394.

98. 104 *Congressional Record,* 85th Cong., 2nd Sess. (1958), 13347.

99. 103 *Congressional Record,* 85th Cong., 1st Sess. (1957), A7427.

100. 104 *Congressional Record,* 85th Cong., 2nd Sess. (1958), 7846.

101. *Ibid.,* 7844. Since the focus of this study is on judicial *criticism,* the role of the Court's defenders has not been emphasized.

NOTES TO CHAPTER 4

1. The basis for selecting the organizations examined was predicated upon practical considerations rather than a scientific sampling. An attempt was made to secure as

much literature and information as possible from a list of ultra-conservative organizations compiled from an examination of the *Congressional Record,* congressional hearing reports, popular news magazines, journals, and bibliographies. The material received from the respective organizations has been utilized to the fullest throughout the chapter. Where the information from a particular organization appears limited, it is due either to the restricted role the organization apparently exercised with respect to the Court controversy, or to a reluctance on the part of that organization to provide the author with the requested information. It appeared that all groups cooperated as best they could.

2. Robert Welch, *The Blue Book of the John Birch Society* (Belmont, 1961), p. ii.

3. *Encyclopedia of Associations,* Vol. I (Detroit, 1961), p. 635.

4. Robert Welch, *American Opinion* (January, 1961), p. 10.

5. Robert Welch, "The Movement to Impeach Earl Warren," *American Opinion* (Supplement to February Bulletin, 1961), 1.

6. Robert Welch, *American Opinion* (January, 1961), 11.

7. "Speak to God's Children...Move Forward," Taken from an appeal for funds to establish a summer anti-Communist youth university, mimeographed (July, 1962).

8. M.T. Phelps, "Danger Confronting the United States," *Weekly Crusader* (Feb. 16, 1962), p. 1.

9. Billy James Hargis, "Supreme Court," *Christian Crusade* — Television No. 4 (Mimeographed).

10. *Ibid., Communist America — Must It Be* (Tulsa, 1960).

11. Hargis, "Supreme Court," 3.

12. *Manion Forum Network,* Weekly Broadcast No. 252 (July 26, 1959), 4.

13. *Manion Forum Network,* Weekly Broadcast No. 251 (July 19, 1959), 4.

14. U. S., Congress, Senate, Internal Security Subcommittee, *Hearings on S.* 2646, 85th Cong., 2nd Sess. (1958), 583.

15. 102 *Congressional Record,* 84th Cong., 2nd Sess. (1956), A2717.

16. *Ibid.,* A3080.

17. *Ibid.,* A3081.

18. *Hearings on S.* 2646, Appendix IV.

19. *Ibid.,* 1079.

20. *Ibid.,* 70.

21. See the following *Economic Council Letters:* "To the Democratic and Republican National Conventions," Letter No. 389 (Aug. 18, 1956), "The Mason Treaty Power Amendment," Letter No. 410 (July 1, 1957), "The Supreme Court of the United States — Do Communist Influences Mold Its Decisions?", Letter No. 482 (July 1, 1957), and "Where We Stand Today," Letter No. 487 (Sept. 15, 1960).

22. *Economic Council Letter,* "The Mason Treaty Power Amendment," 3.

23. *Ibid.,* 4.

24. *Idem.*

25. *Ibid.,* 2.

26. *Hearings on S.* 2646, 104.

27. *Ibid.,* 312.

28. *Ibid.,* 173.

29. *Ibid.,* 231.

30. *Independent American* (Feb.-Mar., 1962), 1.

31. *Tax-Fax* No. 5 (1959).

32. *Tax-Fax* No. 27 (1961).

33. There were no data available as to the number of people the *Independent American* reached.

34. *Dan Smoot Report,* Broadcast 287 (Jan. 30, 1961).

35. See Fred J. Cook, "The Ultras," *Nation* (June 30, 1962), p. 573 *et seq.,* an excellent discussion of this issue. It is estimated that the business community contributed about $10 million to the Radical Right in 1961.

36. Rosalie Gordon, *Nine Men Against America* (New York, 1960).

37. *Ibid.,* 29.

38. *Ibid.,* 53.

39. David Lawrence, *Supreme Court or Political Puppets* (N.Y., 1937).

40. *Ibid.,* "Twenty Years of Court Packing," *U.S. News and World Report,* XVL (Dec. 12, 1958), 116.

41. 106 *Congressional Record,* 86th Cong., 2nd Sess. (1960), 4509.

42. At the top of the editorial page may be found the following statement: "This page presents the opinion of the Editor. The news pages are written by other staff members independently of these editorial views."

43. *U.S. News and World Report,* XVL (Dec. 12, 1958), 116.

44. *Ibid.,* XIIL (June 28, 1957), 152.

45. *Ibid.,* XL (June 1, 1956), 36.

46. "Investigate Supreme Court Law Clerk System," *Ibid.,* XIVL (May 16, 1958), 117.

47. "The Court Must be Curbed," *Ibid.,* XL (May 18, 1956), 50.

48. *Ibid.,* XVL (Oct. 24, 1958), 36.

49. *Ibid.,* XIIIL (Dec. 13, 1957), 74.

50. *Hearings on S.* 2646, 840.

51. *National Review* (July 6, 1957), 6.

52. "Supreme Court on Security," *National Review* (Feb. 15, 1958), 159.

53. "Should We Impeach Earl Warren," *Ibid.,* (Sept. 9, 1961), 153.

54. *Ibid.,* (July 20, 1957), 83.

55. *Ibid.,* (Sept. 7, 1957), 201.

56. *Ibid.,* (Mar. 1, 1958), 200.

57. *Ibid.,* (Sept. 11, 1956), 14.

58. This figure appears to be especially high for this type of a publication.

59. Thomas J. Anderson, "Straight Talk," *Farm and Ranch Magazine* (Sept. 1957), p. 17.

60. *New York Herald Tribune* (June 5, 1957), as cited in Walter Murphy, *Congress and the Court* (Chicago, 1962), p. 113.

61. *Chicago New World* (June 21, 1957), p. 19.

62. 103 *Congressional Record,* 85th Cong., 1st Sess. (1957), A4931.

63. See Walter Murphy, *Congress and the Court* (Chicago, 1962), pp. 112-114, and pp. 128-130.

64. See *New York Times* (June 29, 1962), 11, for numerous excerpts of editorial comment on this issue.

65. *American Legion Magazine* (Nov., 1957), 35.

66. J. B Mathews, "Relief for American Reds," *American Legion Magazine* (Oct., 1957), 15.

67. *Ibid.,* 44.

68. *Ibid.*, (Oct., 1959), 18.

69. *Firing Line*, VII, No. 4 (Feb. 15, 1958).

70. *New York Times* (April 17, 1958), 32.

71. *Hearings on S.* 2646, 113.

72. *Ibid.*, 134.

73. Murphy, p. 202 *et seq.*

74. *New York Times* (Jan 4, 1958), 30.

75. *Ibid.*, (June 17, 1962), 21.

76. *Idem.*

77. *Idem.*

78. *Ibid.*, (Aug. 3, 1962), 7.

NOTES TO CHAPTER 5

1. 339 *U.S.* 629 (1950).

2. 339 *U.S.* 637 (1950).

3. 103 *Congressional Record*, 85th Cong., 1st Sess. (1957), 243.

4. *Ibid.*, 1616.

5. *Ibid.*, 9070.

6. *Ibid.*, 243.

7. *Ibid.*, A4218.

8. *New York Times* (May 19, 1954), 1.

9. 103 *Congressional Record*, 85th Cong., 1st Sess. (1957), A4219.

10. *Georgia Laws*, H. Res. 185 (1956).

11. *Virginia Acts of Assembly*, S. J. Res. 3 (1956).

12. *Mississippi General Laws*, S. Con. Res. 125 (1956).

13. *Acts of Alabama*, No. 42 (1956).

14. *Acts of South Carolina* (Feb. 14, 1956), 1 *Race Rel. L. Rep.* 443 (1956).

15. 103 *Congressional Record*, 85th Cong., 1st Sess. (1957), 244.

16. 350 *U.S.* 497 (1956).

17. 102 *Congressional Record*, 85th Cong., 2nd Sess. (1956), 12410.

18. *New York Times* (July 4, 1962), 1. Governor Rockefeller of New York claimed that he abstained in the voice vote on this resolution.

19. The National Association of Attorney Generals might also be cited as a state critic, but they have not really contributed that much to the anti-Court cause. The N.A.A.G. did endorse H. R. 3 in 1955, and New Hampshire's Attorney General, Louis Wyman, has delivered several speeches before the N.A.A.G. and other organizations taking the Court to task, but this about constitutes the extent of the association's role.

20. 8 *U. of Chi. Law School Rec.* (Spec. Supp., 1958). See John R. Schmidhauser, *The Supreme Court — Its Politics, Personalities, and Procedures* (New York, 1960), for a more detailed discussion of this problem.

21. *Report of the Conference of State Chief Justices*, 1958 (Richmond, 1958), 5.

22. *Ibid.*, 9.

23. *Ibid.*, 36.

24. *Ibid.*, 9.

25. *Ibid.*, 36.

26. See William B. Lockhart, "A Response to the Conference of State Chief Justices," 107 *U. of Pa. L. Rev.* 802 (1959); John R. Schmidhauser, *The Supreme Court — Its Politics, Personalities, and Procedures* (N.Y., 1960), 92; Paul Freund, *The Supreme Court of the United States, Its Business, Purpose and Performance* (N.Y., 1961), 178; and Harold W. Chase, "The Warren Court and Congress," 44 *Minne. L. Rev.* 595 (1960).

27. Lockhart, 804.

28. Schmidhauser, pp. 83-88.

29. Chase, 598.

30. The Jenner bill, which was under consideration in 1958, had previously offered an opportunity for a wealth of varied attacks upon the Court.

NOTES TO CHAPTER 6

1. U.S., Congress, Senate, Subcommittee on Constitutional Rights, "Confessions and Police Detection," *Hearings on S. Res.* 234 (1958).

2. *Ibid.*, 124.

3. *Ibid.*, 125.

4. *Idem.*

5. *New York Times* (Oct. 6, 1957), 62.

6. *Idem.*

7. *Idem.*

8. 103 *Congressional Record*, 85th Cong., 1st Sess. (1957), A6562.

9. *Hearings on S. Res.* 234, 24.

10. *Ibid.*, 595.

11. *Ibid.*, 599.

12. *New York Times* (July 29, 1957), 12.

13. *Idem.*

14. *Idem.*

15. 103 *Congressional Record*, 85th Cong., 1st Sess. (1957), 16119.

16. *Idem.* See Murphy, pp. 139-140 for a more detailed description of the lobbying activities of the F.B.I.

17. 103 *Congressional Record*, 85th Cong., 1st Sess. (1957), A6638.

18. *Idem.*

19. *Hearings on S. Res.* 234, 136.

20. *Mapp v. Ohio,* 367 *U.S.* 643 (1961).

21. 338 *U.S.* 25 (1949).

22. 232 *U.S.* 383 (1914).

23. 347 *U.S.* 23 (1963).

24. 372 *U.S.* 335 (1963).

25. 287 *U.S.* 45 (1932).

26. 316 *U.S.* 455 (1942).

27. *Palko v. Connecticut,* 302 *U.S.* 319 (1937).

28. Anthony Lewis, *Gideon's Trumpet* (New York: 1964).

29. 377 *U.S.* 201 (1964).

30. 378 *U.S.* 478 (1964).

31. *Powell v. Alabama,* 287 *U.S.* 45, 57 (1932).

32. *Boston Evening Globe* (July 14, 1964), p. 26.

33. *New York Times* (May 14, 1965), p. 39.

34. See *Twining v. New Jersey*, 211 *U.S.* 78 (1908).

35. 378 *U.S.* 1 (1964).

36. 13. *L. Ed.* 2d. 923 (1965).

37. 14 *L. Ed.* 2d. 106 (1965).

38. 86 *S. Ct.* 1602, (1966). The other three cases were *Vignera v. New York, California v. Stewart,* and *Westover v. United States.* All four cases fall under the same citation.

39. Actually Mr. Justice Clark concurred with the majority in *California v. Stewart,* but not on substantive grounds.

40. 86 *S. Ct.* 1602, 1612 (1966).

41. *Idem.*

42. *Idem.*

43. *Ibid.*, 1623.

44. 378 *U.S.* 1, 8 (1964).

45. 86 *S. Ct.*, 1602, 1642 (1966).

46. *Ibid.*, 1641.

47. *Ibid.*, 1663.

48. *Idem.*

49. *Ibid.*, 1643.

50. *Ibid.*, 1650.

51. *Ibid.*, 1664-65.

52. *Christian Science Monitor* (June 16, 1966), p. 12.

53. *Christian Science Monitor* (June 15, 1966), p. 5.

54. *Idem.*

55. From an interview with Mr. Schafer on July 29, 1966, in Tucson, Arizona.

56. *Christian Science Monitor* (June 15, 1966), p. 5.

57. *Christian Science Monitor* (June 16, 1966), p. 12.

58. 86 *S. Ct.* 1772 (1966).

59. *Christian Science Monitor* (May 2, 1966), p. 9.

60. Quoted in an article by Fred Sondern, "Take the Handcuffs Off Our Police," *Reader's Digest,* Vol. 85 (Sept., 1964), p. 64, at p. 65.

61. *Ibid.*, at p. 66.

62. *Christian Science Monitor* (May 2, 1966), p. 9.

63. *Pittsburgh Post Gazette* (May 8, 1964), p. 7.

64. Scileppi, John F., "Is Society Shortchanged at the Bar of Justice," F.B.I.: *Law Enforcement Bulletin* (May, 1964), p. 7.

65. *New York Times* (Sept. 16, 1964), p. 1.

66. *Journal of Criminal Law, Criminology, and Police Science,* Vol. 53, No. 1 (1962), pp. 85-89.

67. *Ibid.*, at p. 86.

68. *Ibid.*, at p. 89.

69. Yale Kamisar, "Public Safety v. Individual Liberties: Some 'Facts' and Theories," *Journal of Criminal Law, Criminology and Police Science,* Vol. 53, No. 2 (1962), pp. 171-193.

70. 318 *U.S.* 332 (1943).

71. 232 *U.S.* 383 (1914).

72. Yale Kamisar, "Some Reflections on Criticizing The Courts and Policing The Police," *Journal of Criminal Law, Criminology and Police Science*, Vol. 53, No. 4 (1962), p. 453 at p. 454-455. See also Fred Inbau's second article of the debate entitled "More About Public Safety v. Individual Liberties," *Ibid.*, Vol. 53, No. 3 (1962), pp. 329-332.

73. *New York Times* (Aug. 30, 1963), p. 13.

74. H. Alan Long "The Dilemma: Crime and Constitutional Rights," *The Police Chief* (June, 1965), pp. 14-22.

75. *Christian Science Monitor* (May 2, 1966), p. 9.

76. *Idem.*

77. *The Police Chief* (Dec., 1965), p. 24.

78. *Police Training Bulletin*, Vol. 4, No. 2 (1965), p. 1.

NOTES TO CHAPTER 7

1. *U.S. News and World Report*, XL (May 18, 1956), 50.

2. *Ibid.*, 58.

3. See 104 *Congressional Record*, 85th Cong., 2nd Sess. (1958), 7234, for several reprints of speeches made before local bar associations.

4. *Journal of Politics*, IXX (Feb., 1957), 81.

5. 314 *U.S.* 160 (1941).

6. U.S., Congress, Senate, Internal Security Subcommittee, *Hearings on S.* 2646, 85th Cong., 2nd Sess. (1958), 170.

7. Walter B. Jones, "Selection of U.S. Supreme Court Judges," *Montgomery Advertiser* (June 14, 1957), 7.

8. Marlin T. Phelps, "Supreme Court — Communists' Most Precious Asset," *Manion Forum*, Weekly Broadcast No. 307 (Aug. 14, 1960), 2.

9. *Ibid.*, 2.

10. *Ibid.*, 4.

11. John R. Dethmers, "What a State Chief Justice Says About the Supreme Court," *U.S. News and World Report*, XVL (Dec. 12, 1958), 88.

12. Dozier DeVane, "A Federal Judge Starts a Crusade," *U.S. News and World Report*, XVL (Dec. 26, 1958), 67.

13. Freund, Sutherland, Howe and Brown, *Constitutional Law: Cases and Other Problems* (Boston, 1961), 1v.

14. 321 *U.S.* 649, 669 (1944).

15. *Baker v. Carr*, 369 *U.S.* 186 (1962).

16. Robert H. Jackson, *The Struggle for Judicial Supremacy* (N.Y. 1941), 321.

17. *United States v. Butler*, 297 *U.S.* 1, 79 (1936).

18. 105 *Congressional Record*, 86th Cong., 1st Sess. (1959), 3362. For resolutions of local and state bar associations, see: 104 *Congressional Record*, 85th Cong., 2nd Sess. (1958), 12921 — Phila.; *ibid.*, 9657 — St. Louis; *ibid.*, 13319 — Oklahoma; *ibid.*, 14537 — North Dakota; *ibid.*, 18022 — Michigan.

19. *American Bar Association*, Canons of Professional Ethics 1 (1908).

20. 103 *Congressional Record*, 85th Cong., 1st Sess. (1957), 13286.

21. *Ibid.*, A859.

22. *Hearings on S.* 2646, 359.

23. 45 *A.B.A.J.* 406-410 (1959).

24. *Idem.*

25. John Schmidhauser, *The Supreme Court — Its Politics, Personalities, and Procedures* (N.Y., 1960), p. 71 *et seq.*

26. *Ibid.*, p. 77.

27. See Phillip Kurland, "The Supreme Court and Its Judicial Critics," 6 *Utah L. Rev.* 457 (1959), and Paul Freund, "The Supreme Court Crisis," 3 *N.Y. State Bar Bull,* 66 (1959).

28. John E. Nolan, "Supreme Court versus A.B.A.," *Commonweal,* LXX (May 15, 1959), 179.

29. 105 *Congressional Record,* 86th Cong., 1st Sess. (1959), 3373.

30. *Ibid.*, 3379.

31. *New York Times* (Mar. 5, 1959), 14.

32. Kurland, 457.

33. *New York Times* (Aug. 7, 1962), 1.

34. *Ibid.* (Aug. 10, 1962), 16.

35. Harold Chase, "The Warren Court and Congress," 44 *Minne. L. Rev.* 595 (1960).

36. Arthur J. Keefe, "Comments on the Supreme Court's Treatment of the Bill of Rights in the October Term, 1956," 26 *Fordham L. Rev.* 468 (1957).

37. Robert G. McCloskey, "Deeds Without Doctrines: Civil Rights in the 1960 Term of the Supreme Court," *A.P.S.R.,* LXI (1962), 71.

38. Fred Rodell, *Nine Men* (New York, 1955), p. 23.

39. Herbert Wechsler, "Toward Neutral Principles in Constitutional Law," 73 *Harv. L. Rev.* 1 (1959).

40. Learned Hand, *The Bill of Rights* (Cambridge, 1958).

41. *Ibid.*, 55.

42. *Ibid.*, 15.

43. *Ibid.*, 55.

44. Wechsler, 15.

45. *Idem.*

46. Louis H. Pollak, "Racial Discrimination and Judicial Integrity; A Reply to Professor Wechsler," 108 *U. of Pa. L. Rev.* 1 (1959).

47. Louis Henkin, "Some Reflections on Current Constitutional Controversy," 109 *U. of Pa. L. Rev.* 637 (1961).

48. *Ibid.*, 655.

49. *Ibid.*, 661.

50. Addison Mueller and Murray Schwartz, "The Principle of Neutral Principles," 7 *U.C.L.A.L. Rev.* 571 (1960).

51. Arthur S. Miller and Ronald S. Howell, "The Myth of Neutrality in Constitutional Adjudication," 27 *U. of Chi. L. Rev.* 661 (1960).

52. *Ibid.*, 690-691.

53. Benjamin F. Wright, "The Supreme Court Cannot Be Neutral," delivered at the 1961 annual meeting of the American Political Science Association (mimeographed).

54. *Ibid.*, 12.

55. *Watkins v. United States,* 354 *U.S.* 178 (1957), *Yates v. United States,* 354 *U.S.* 298 (1957), *Sweezy v. New Hampshire,* 354 *U.S.* 234 (1957), and *Service v. Dulles,* 354 *U.S.* 363 (1957).

56. *New York Times* (April 19, 1957), 20.

57. Edward S. Corwin, *The Constitution and What It Means Today*, 12th ed. (Princeton, 1957).

58. *New York Times* (Mar. 16, 1958), IV, 10.

59. *Idem.*

60. Henry M. Hart, Jr., "The Supreme Court 1958 Term — Foreword: The Time Chart of the Justices," 73 *Harv. L. Rev.* 84 (1959-60).

61. *Ibid.*, 100.

62. Thurman Arnold, "Professor Hart's Theology," 73 *Harv. L. Rev.* 1298 (1959-60).

63. *Ibid.*, 1312.

64. Erwin Griswold, "Foreword: Of Time and Attitudes — Professor Hart and Judge Arnold," 74 *Harv. L. Rev.* 81 (1960).

65. *Ibid.*, 84.

66. Paul Freund, *The Supreme Court of the United States* (Cleveland, 1961), p. 184.

67. *Ibid.*, 188.

68. *Idem.*

69. McCloskey, 88.

70. Ernest Brown, "Foreword: Process of Law, the Supreme Court 1957 Term," 72 *Harv. L. Rev.* 77 (1958).

71. Alexander Bickel and Harry Wellington, "Legislative Purpose and the Judicial Procedure: The Lincoln Mills Case," 71 *Harv. L. Rev.* 1 (1957).

72. *Ibid.*, 3.

73. *Ibid.*, 4.

NOTES TO CHAPTER 8

1. *Baker v. Carr*, 369 U. S. 186 (1962), *Wesberry v. Sanders*, 376 U. S. 1 (1964), *Reynolds v. Simms*, 84 S. Ct. 1362 (1964).

2. *Engel v. Vitale*, 370 U.S. 421 (1962). Also see *Abington School District v. Schempp*. 374 U. S. 203 (1963).

3. "Congressional Reversal of Supreme Court Decisions: 1945-1957," 71 Harv. L. Rev. 1324 (1958).

4. *Ibid.*, 1336.

5. 103 *Congressional Record*, 85th Cong., 1st Sess. (1957), 10543.

INDEX OF CASES

GENERAL INDEX